I've travelled the world twice over,
Met the famous: saints and sinners,
Poets and artists, kings and queens,
Old stars and hopeful beginners,
I've been where no-one's been before,
Learned secrets from writers and cooks
All with one library ticket
To the wonderful world of books.

© JANICE JAMES.

LIZA MINNELLI

Liza Minnelli is one of the world's most exciting talents. Daughter of Hollywood legend Judy Garland, her traumatic childhood was the prelude to a continuing battle to be recognized as a legitimate talent in her own right. At 19 she became the youngest performer to win Broadway's Tony Award. She scaled the heights in the phenomenally successful *Cabaret*, for which she won the Best Actress Oscar. She is equally compelling in film and on television, as a recording artist and in cabaret, concert and theatre. This revealing biography not only documents her professional life, but provides a unique focus to this highly charged, emotional performer.

PETER CARRICK

LIZA MINNELLI

Complete and Unabridged

ULVERSCROFT
Leicester

First published in Great Britain in 1993 by
Robert Hale Limited
London

First Large Print Edition
published March 1995
by arrangement with
Robert Hale Limited
London

British Library CIP Data

Carrick, Peter
Liza Minnelli.—Large print ed.—
Ulverscroft large print series: non-fiction
I. Title
791.43028092

ISBN 0–7089–3254–1

Published by
F. A. Thorpe (Publishing) Ltd.
Anstey, Leicestershire
Set by Words & Graphics Ltd.
Anstey, Leicestershire
Printed and bound in Great Britain by
T. J. Press (Padstow) Ltd., Padstow, Cornwall

This book is printed on acid-free paper

To Brenda especially . . .

but also for Sarah, Debbie, Vaughan, Alan, Adam, Chloe, Sam and Harry

Acknowledgements

A number of people were of considerable help when I was researching this biography of Liza Minnelli. I would like to thank Sir John Gielgud and Tim Rice; Ron Millett, Peter Cliffe and Keith Jarvis; the information staff at the British Film Institute and the Mander and Mitchenson Theatre Collection; the editorial department of the *Stage* and *Television Today*; and American Express Europe Limited.

My special gratitude is extended to Graham Jackson, one of the most knowledgeable sources of information on Liza Minnelli in the UK, and to Laura Elston, the European chapterhead of *Limelight on Liza*. Their patience and understanding in answering my questions and providing evidence and information was unstinting. Additionally, my thanks go to Graham for providing most of the information for the video and audio listings at the end of the book.

For his encouragement and support during my early work on the book I am grateful to my old colleague and dear friend David Boyce, who sadly died before publication.

For permission to reproduce short extracts from published material I am grateful to Virgin Publishing (*Liza with a Z* by Michael Freedland and *Liza: Her Cinderella Nightmare* by James Robert Parish and Jack Arno); Sidgwick & Jackson (*Judy and Liza* by James Spada and Karen Swenson); Rogers, Coleridge & White Ltd (*Judy Garland* by Anne Edwards); Robson Books (*My Side of the Road* by Dorothy Lamour with Dick McInnes); Random House Inc (*The Poet at the Piano* by Michiko Kakutani); Mirror Group Newspapers; *Daily Mail*; *Film Review*; the *Observer*; Little, Brown (*The Great Movie Stars* by David Shipman); Orbis Publishing (*The Movie*); HarperCollins (*Halliwell's Film Guide* edited by John Walker); Bison Group (*History of Movie Musicals* by Thomas G. Aylesworth); and the Octopus Publishing Group (*The Paramount Story* by John Douglas Eames).

Additional sources of information and verification were *Limelight on Liza*, *Films and Filming*, *Photoplay*, *The United Artists Story*, *Judy* by Gerold Frank (Harper & Row), the *Guardian*, *Sunday Times*, *The Times*, *Newsweek*, *Good Housekeeping*, *Première* magazine, *Celebrity Spotlight*, *Variety*, *Hello* magazine, *Network*, *New Yorker*, *Harper's Bazaar*, BBC TV, London Weekend Television and TVam.

1

A Swinging Match for Mama

LIZA had taken the surprise call from London while she was battling to get her stage career off the ground. She was at first opposed to her mother's idea that they should appear together at Britain's famous London Palladium. For one thing she hated the mock sentimentality which invariably crept into a 'mother and daughter' act, though it wouldn't have been the first time that they had worked together. For another she was fiercely independent, intent on making her name as Liza Minnelli and not Judy Garland's daughter.

But Judy, for her own reasons as well as for the timely boost it would give to Liza's emerging career, was determined. She chose to ignore what Liza had said and went ahead with the arrangements just the same. Then told the London papers all about it. Judy was so popular in Britain that, without being advertized, the Judy and Liza show at the country's premier variety theatre was totally sold out within two days. A second performance was hastily arranged to take place a week after the first.

The year was 1964. Liza was eighteen years old and, as had happened often before, Judy was once again calling the shots. When Judy spoke to her daughter again she ignored Liza's earlier protestations, rhetorically announcing that wasn't it great that all the tickets had been sold? Meanwhile Liza had given the idea second thoughts. She was ambitious to move her career forward as quickly as possible and recognized just how important it would be to share the spotlight with her mother at the Palladium. She was happy enough to put aside her earlier doubts and was excited and enthusiastic, if a little intimidated, at the prospect.

Liza Minnelli was finding it hard to kick-start her career in show business. She had decided rather late to follow the family tradition, bearing in mind that she was the daughter of Hollywood superstar Judy Garland and Vincente Minnelli, a successful director of screen musicals. She had appeared as a toddler in one of their pictures, and her first ambition was to be a dancer. She had been doing well in a major part in an off-Broadway revival of *Best Foot Forward* but when she left the show which closed after a near seven-month run on 13 October 1963, she found it hard to keep up the momentum. Meantime her single recording of 'You Are For Loving' from *Best Foot Forward* was selling well, getting her name established with the public.

In contrast Judy's career was past its best, even as a theatre performer. It had been ten years since her outstanding portrayal as overnight singing sensation Esther Blodgett (renamed Vicki Lester) in the film *A Star is Born*, widely considered by critics and movie-goers alike to be the peak of her mature screen career. During that time the personal drink and drug problems which had bedevilled her for years had sadly shown no signs of improvement.

In 1964 she had decided to spend some time in London, but still bore the emotional scars of a recent turbulent and torrid time in Australia and Hong Kong. Her concert in Sydney had been a triumph, but Melbourne turned into a nightmare. Some sources put the problem down to her drugs being confiscated on arrival in Australia. She knew she couldn't perform without them and panicked until further supplies were obtained for her indirectly from a dubious local source. Other reports were more generous, attributing her condition to the intense fatigue of her long-haul flight to Australia combined with her fear of flying.

Whatever the truth of the matter, Judy was physically and mentally drained as the Melbourne concert approached. To give her the boost she needed to perform before a huge crowd in a large outdoor arena, she took a liberal dose of amphetamine. This made her unsteady and shaky when walking and moving, which not only led to her being an hour late for the concert, but was easily noticed by the audience.

The outcome was a sad and embarrassing spectacle. She stumbled over the microphone, missed cues, sang poorly and had difficulty with some of the words. In such a dire situation she did well to continue for more than half an hour and, in truth, her personality, stage presence and experience disguised from the audience some of the more depressing elements of this pitiful display. But they continued to resent her late appearance and after being numbed and shocked they grew angry, thinking she was drunk. As Judy continued, the audience threw insults and shouted abuse, until she finally put down the microphone and fled the stage.

Humiliated, she left the country, after being booed at the airport, and was still psychologically spent on arrival in Hong Kong, where she had decided to break her journey. A bumpy flight from Australia did nothing for her composure and she felt no better even when safely checked into her hotel. But there was to be little respite for the suffering Judy. A severe storm battered the colony and, stricken once more with fear, she insisted she be left alone to rest.

Mark Herron, an undistinguished actor ten years her junior whom she would soon marry, had accompanied her on the concert tour as a kind of manager, administrator and general companion. When later he checked to see if she wanted anything he found her unconscious. Unable to rouse her, he called for help and an ambulance rushed her to a local hospital. She had been in a coma for some considerable time. They pumped her stomach and at one point a nurse announced that she was dead. But after fifteen hours they managed to revive her.

The word was quickly out that she had taken a drug overdose by mistake and shock reports of her 'death' even reached the United States, causing a fleeting moment of panic. The hospital authorities in Hong Kong denied she had suffered an overdose, or that a heart attack had been responsible for her condition. Total exhaustion might have triggered off the collapse, because although her bodyweight could oscillate between a shadowy, almost skeletal, 85 lb and a ballooning 195 lb, she was at this point in her life a frail beanpole weighing less than 90 lb at a height of 5 ft 2 in. Once sufficiently recovered to travel, Judy decided to spend the summer of 1964 in London, where she was twice more ill, spending time as an inpatient at a private nursing home.

In Britain, Judy Garland had been a traditional favourite for years. The public had read about her fight against pill and drink dependency and her reported suicide attempts with compassion, deep sorrow and tolerance. They looked back with undiminished affection to those early MGM musicals with Mickey Rooney and her captivating performance as Dorothy in the magical *The Wizard of Oz*, which had done its part in helping to brighten the spectre of those early years of the war.

They showed they had lost none of their affection for her when she visited the Palladium in the July of 1964, having been invited to the glittering *Night of a Thousand Stars*, the country's most glamorous and important single charity event. She defied her doctors in going, but made it clear she was not well enough to sing; she would simply appear on stage to say hello to the distinguished audience. But when she stepped out from the wings the reception was so great and the calls for her to sing so insistent that, filled with emotion, she finally capitulated. With the microphone in her hand, sitting on the edge of the stage, she sang 'Over the Rainbow' from *The Wizard of Oz* which had long since become her trademark song, and then the old Al Jolson number, 'Swanee'. It was particularly moving and the audience gave her a deep and enthusiastic ovation.

Liza had become aware of these unfolding dramas, but from America could do little to help or support her mother. In any event, by this time the crazy ups and downs of Garland's life style had become routine. So it was no surprise to Liza, when she arrived in London towards the end of October to keep the Palladium date with her mother, to find her still suffering indifferent health, both physically and emotionally. She had grown up with such uncertainties and, in more recent years, had suffered

Judy's often tiresome meddling in her life. Two years before, as a 16-year-old, she had broken away from Judy's oppressive influence and headed for New York and the bright lights of Broadway. Since then they had not seen a lot of each other, though there had been frequent contact, each of their lives having a bearing, if little influence, on the other.

London was not new to Liza: as a child she had accompanied her mother to Europe and witnessed some of her most notable triumphs. But her recent decision to join Judy for the Palladium concerts had made little impact in Britain. Audiences were impatient to show their continued loyalty to the Hollywood legend and had besieged the box office because they wanted to see Judy, not her daughter Liza Minnelli.

This was hardly surprising since Liza was little known even in her own country, and hardly at all in the UK. But Judy had her reasons for inviting Liza. After the trauma of Melbourne and Hong Kong, and despite her two-song triumph at the Palladium variety show four months before, she had little confidence in being able to sustain a two-hour performance at one of the world's most famous variety theatres without help of some kind. Yet she was desperate to rekindle something of her disintegrating career. This was the prime reason, some cynics would suggest, for Judy's conspiratorial invitation to Liza. With Liza on stage to handle some of the show, she felt confident she could make a success of it.

Liza herself probably suspected a hidden motive, as their relationship over the years had veered through extremes of love, resentment, bitterness and indifference. Yet they always made up in the end and as time went on Liza resolutely defended her mother against almost every scrap of outside criticism. But she was only too well aware of the difficulties which could arise from her mother's interference in her life. It had been hard to come to terms with the brutal fact that the scant career openings which had come her way were most likely because she was Judy Garland's daughter. Yet not long before her mother's ill-fated visit to Australia, Liza's determination had led to her being offered a star part in a stock production of the successful Broadway show, *Carnival*.

Judy was in one of her possessive moods and didn't want her to go, much preferring that Liza remain in California as a companionable stabilizer to her own emotional fluctuations and debilitating bouts of depression. To be fair to Judy, she cared about Liza too, and was genuinely concerned when Liza had earlier suffered kidney stone problems. Liza spent a month in hospital and was still not home when the *Carnival* chance came up. She signed the contract and on leaving hospital went to Long Island to join the cast in rehearsal.

Two months later she was ill again and Judy flew from California to be with her, insisting again that she give up the part. When Liza said she was determined to honour the contract she had signed, Judy flew into a rage and claimed she would do everything possible to stop her from going on. The situation turned uglier as neither would give way. At one point Liza was told during the intermission of one of her performances that there had been a call to say that

Judy had attempted suicide. Not unused by this time to Judy's histrionics, Liza was convinced that many of her mother's so-called suicide attempts were nothing more than a means of gaining attention and, once she was assured that Judy was going to be all right, returned to the show to give what was generally considered to be an outstanding second half performance.

But Judy persisted. Her mood developed to the extent that it was almost a personal vendetta, a crusade which she would later conduct surreptitiously. It was emotionally upsetting for Liza who felt she had her own life to lead yet didn't want to upset her mother. Despite Judy's attitude, Liza was enjoying good notices for her performances and moved with the show to New Jersey where rehearsals were thrown into disarray when a lawyer representing Judy called to say that her mother was taking Liza out of the show because she considered her too young. Fortunately Liza's father heard what was going on and, despite his estrangement from Judy, persuaded her to let their daughter have her chance for a stage career. Judy relented, easing Liza's intense frustration, exasperation and anger.

It was against this agonizing background — for Liza the crippling interference in her career by her mother and for Judy the panicked realization that she was incapable in her present state of carrying a two-hour show on her own — that recent differences were set aside. Other important issues, too, had conspired to bring them together. Liza had recently cut her first LP, *Liza! Liza!*, which incidentally included 'Maybe This Time', soon to become a Minnelli standard, and sent her mother an advance copy. It was a good performance and Judy knew it. She realized, perhaps for the first time, that her daughter had great potential as a singer and this made her feel she wanted to help. Then there was Liza's ambition to further her career. And last, but by no means least, was the plain and harsh truth that both of them could do with the money they would receive from the Palladium engagement.

In the end both seemed genuinely excited about appearing together. It

13

would recharge Judy's emotional batteries, and rebuild her confidence in front of an audience dedicated to the legend of Garland. Liza, sensing the special nature of the occasion, had her friend, the young and as yet undiscovered Marvin Hamlisch, produce some special song arrangements for her.

But that first performance on Sunday, 8 November 1964, was to turn out as neither had expected. At the start Garland was obviously the star and warmly received. Many in the audience remembered with affection her previous outstandingly successful concerts in the UK during the 1950s and '60s, and were eager to show that despite everything she still held a special place in the affections of the British public. Then she introduced her daughter and, as Judy walked off stage, Liza swung into a sensational debut. Polite applause had greeted her first appearance on stage, but this turned into an unexpected and enthusiastic appreciation of her talent as her medley of up-tempo numbers came to an end.

It wasn't long before this Palladium

audience realized they were witnessing a unique event. There was Judy, much loved for her past glories and now a veteran performer with close on thirty years' experience in the business. And there was Liza, the virtually unknown teenager, appearing for the first time at one of the most famous theatres in the world. The audience had come to see Judy; of that there was no doubt. Liza's appearance was a novelty, a bonus if you like, but no more than a novelty all the same. But as the programme developed, Liza's youthful vitality, her strong singing and refreshing stage presence made her the new star of the show. She had a look of the youthful Judy, moved like her, exhibited the same special mannerisms. Liza was on top form, uplifted by appearing for the first time as an artist on equal terms with her mother, and determined to grasp the opportunity to make the audience hers.

Judy was probably not fully recovered from her recent illness and her voice might still have been affected by her hospitalization in Hong Kong. When Judy and Liza shared a song the difference was painfully obvious. Judy tried hard but she missed notes and her voice would fade occasionally. As one commentator suggested: 'It almost wasn't Judy's night.' If the audience had been prepared to admit it, Judy was beginning to look and sound her years, though she was still only forty-two. Liza at eighteen was young, fresh and full of new talent. Judy sensed the competitive edge which had developed between them and tried to keep hold of the audience's loyalty. She resorted to hollow gestures in a futile attempt to demonstrate that she was the established performer, fiddling unnecessarily with Liza's microphone as if to show that her daughter was not yet experienced enough to know about such technicalities.

Liza would have her critics, not for her performance, which could hardly be questioned, but for what they considered to be her almost brazen resolve to make the concert a personal triumph with little concern shown for Mama. There was none of the nerves and apprehension she said she had felt before the show. She was relaxed and full of youthful vitality. She swung through 'Who's Sorry Now?' with such style and feeling that one critic would be moved to make a comparison with the great Ella Fitzgerald; her jazz-inspired interpretation built to an exciting, full-voiced climax. It was much beyond anything Judy could match on the night.

But it would be wrong to suggest that the concert was a disaster for Judy in the style of Melbourne. She was still a legendary star with an enormously devoted following. They wouldn't desert her for an upstart daughter who, however talented, still lacked Judy's experience in getting across to an audience. Yet the show proved that nothing lasts for ever. Judy's star, which had shone so brightly and for so long, was now perhaps beginning to fade. The star which had flickered to life for Liza was already beginning to show a brilliant glow.

That first London Palladium concert in November 1964 might not have converted Liza Minnelli into a superstar overnight, but it convincingly established her credentials for star status. Britain recognized in Liza Minnelli an emerging major new talent. Word quickly spread to America. Before coming to London Liza had been trying for the female lead in the forthcoming Broadway production of *Flora, The Red Menace*. On her return to New York she quickly secured the part. It was to be her debut in professional theatre and her performance brought her the accolade of the Tony award for best musical actress of the year — at nineteen, she was the youngest ever recipient.

For the second Palladium show Judy yielded to the youth and stamina of her daughter, but again seemed irritated by Liza's strong performance. At the end she pushed Liza off the stage, but when she attempted 'Over the Rainbow' during the curtain call her voice couldn't cope and she resorted to asking the audience to sing it to her. 'You know it better than me,' she called out.

The shows had been taped for subsequent showing on television in both the US and UK but, as so often happens, the need to reshape more than two hours of stage entertainment into a shortened television format led to a poor choice of clips being made. The result was something of a shambles which did little to uphold Judy's once proud reputation.

Judy would make little public comment afterwards except to hint that the joint appearance with Liza made her realize for the first time that her daughter was not a child any more and had a mind and a destiny of her own. It also showed in no uncertain way that, despite her famous mother, Liza was developing her own public persona. Liza said it was a turning point in their relationship. 'Mama's competitiveness disappeared immediately after the Palladium performance and she fell into a period of unparalleled motherhood with me,' she said.

This all pointed to a time when Judy Garland would no longer hold the exclusive proprietorial rights to on-stage talent in the family; and it also showed that Liza Minnelli, if still having some way to go in show business, was a single-minded, determined young woman and certainly not her mother's daughter for nothing.

2

Born to be a Star

SONS and daughters of the famous stand to benefit from having a celebrated mother or father. Accepting the individual talent of the Redgrave daughters Vanessa and Lynn, who could say that having Sir Michael as a father was not a help in their chosen professions? Of course it isn't always true. It could be argued that Frank Sinatra Jnr, in some of his recordings and performances, phrased and swung more than his old man. Yet there was never a chance that he would unseat the legend.

Comparison is the anathema of a second generation talent. The bigger the legend, the deeper and darker can be the gloom which threatens to engulf the young performer. Here Liza Minnelli was dealt a double blow at birth. Not only was her mother a monumental talent in movies with an overpowering fame which journeyed with ease from one generation to the next, but her father was one of Hollywood's great directors during its most influential years.

Judy Garland was born of vaudeville stock and was on stage at the age of three. At thirteen she joined MGM, the largest film studio in the world, where her young talent and exuberant personality were shamefully exploited. In puberty they gave her pills to keep down her weight; more pills to keep her going during the tensions and debilitations of almost continuous movie-making. Thus artificially hyped, there would always be yet more pills to calm her when she couldn't sleep at night. Such was the reckless ambition of studio handlers to exploit Judy's enormous box-office talent that at her peak she had no fewer than four major films released in just twelve months.

Born in 1922, she made her movie debut when only fourteen in *Every Sunday* (1936), an MGM young-talent short, alongside Deanna Durbin, who at fifteen not only looked good but could sing popular classics in a genuine adult coloratura soprano voice. Hollywood was desperate to inject new life into the flagging screen musical and found that youth could provide the answer. Inexplicably MGM let Durbin go. Universal snapped her up and her first and second starring pictures — *Three Smart Girls* in 1936 and *One Hundred Men and a Girl* in 1937 — saved the studio from bankruptcy. MGM, however, held on to Garland's contract, at the same time loaning her out to 20th Century Fox who cast her in a college musical called *Pigskin Parade*. But it was cinema idol Clark Gable's thirty-sixth birthday celebration which indirectly led to Judy's movie breakthrough. A special version of the song 'You Made Me Love You' had Garland doing a 'Dear Mr Gable' monologue as a fan of the screen idol. MGM were so impressed they reprised the number for Judy's first major screen triumph in *Broadway Melody of 1938* (released 1937).

When Shirley Temple proved unavailable for the starring part in a new picture, Judy stepped in to take over the role of

Dorothy in the enchanting $2 million technicolour version of *The Wizard of Oz* released in 1939. Her touching and sensitive rendition of 'Over the Rainbow' from this most enduring and colourful of all fantasy films made it a song which would become forever closely associated with Garland.

The 17-year-old was by now a movie sensation, having already struck up a spirited, swinging and exuberant partnership with her youthful contemporaries Mickey Rooney in *Thoroughbreds Don't Cry* in 1937 and Freddie Bartholomew in *Listen, Darling* in 1938. She teamed with Mickey Rooney in a series of outstandingly successful features including *Strike Up the Band* and *Babes in Arms*, about talented teenagers putting on backstage musical shows. These became musical classics, as did *Meet Me in St Louis* in 1944, in which she sang another Garland immortal, 'The Trolley Song'. She was by now universally adored for her extraordinary voice, the freshness and vitality of her dancing, her natural effervescence and above all, perhaps, for her uncomplicated, innocent and youthful screen persona.

Still only twenty-two in 1944, she was already the veteran of almost twenty major feature films, and the tragedy of Judy Garland had already begun. The degradation of rigid diet regimes, pep pills and sleeping pills was taking its physical and mental toll, leading to serious addiction and, in 1950, to the first of a number of suicide attempts when she was only twenty-eight.

It was during the making of the smash hit *Meet Me in St Louis* that Judy (as the star) first got to know Vincente Minnelli (as the director), though they had worked together when Minnelli handled some of the scenes in Garland's earlier successes, *Babes in Arms* in 1939 and *Strike Up the Band* in 1940. The son of an Italian violinist and a French opera singer, he was almost 12 years older than Judy and already an outstanding stylist among film-makers, an Academy Award winner in the making. Like Judy, his family was in vaudeville and he graduated to films through the theatre, designing sets and costumes for Broadway shows during the 1930s.

He became a film director at Paramount and as musicals grew popular, a trend which Paramount seemed slow to exploit, a move to MGM was welcomed. Here he could work closely with gifted producer Arthur Freed and was able to indulge his innovative approach by bringing music and story closer together in a number of highly successful musical movies. Starring Garland in the lead role as Esther Smith, *Meet Me in St Louis* was a notable Minnelli triumph, advancing the then new concept of the musical content of the picture coming from the characters as a natural development of the story. This tender family tale of American provincial life at the turn of the century became a classic of its kind.

After Judy's earlier successes in a series of youthful pictures with a strong musical content, and the first and second offerings in what would become the famous Andy Hardy series, MGM had wanted to keep the pot boiling, trying to ward off her growing maturity (by binding her growing breasts tightly for *The Wizard of Oz*, for example). After completing four more pictures, no fewer than three being released in 1940 alone, she eloped in 1941 with composer and orchestra leader David Rose, mostly noted for his recording of 'Holiday For Strings'. The studio bosses did little to hide their displeasure, though in the end MGM reluctantly gave permission. Rose had previously been married to Martha Raye; his marriage to Judy did not last and the pair separated, but not before Judy, still only nineteen, had an abortion.

When *Meet Me in St Louis* was released in 1944 it showed the then 22-year-old Garland to be a seasoned, refined performer and the picture brought Judy some of her most memorable songs including 'Have Yourself a Merry Little Christmas', the title song and the aforementioned 'The Trolley Song'.

She and Minnelli had been distant and disagreeable with one another when they first came together to make the picture, quarrelling over the merits of the plot and the picture itself. Minnelli, though gentle and mild-mannered in private life, could be strong-willed as a director and would often instruct a certain scene to be done over and over again, even when

Judy felt confident it was as good as she could make it. But the tensions between them gradually disappeared, they began dating, and by the time the picture was completed in April 1944 they were living together. After sharing two more pictures — *Ziegfeld Follies* and *The Clock*, the latter giving Judy her first non-singing dramatic casting — her divorce from David Rose became final. Within days, on 15 June 1945, she and Vincente were married and at breakfast time on Tuesday, 12 March 1946 at the Cedars of Lebanon Hospital in Hollywood, their daughter was delivered by Caesarian section. She weighed 6 lb 10½ oz.

Her pregnancy was probably the happiest few months of Judy's chaotic life. Without studio commitments, though she was at the height of her career when her daughter was born, Judy was able to relax, and according to some reports managed to live without all the pills which earlier had become habitual. Both parents were overjoyed at having a daughter. They named her Liza May. Liza came from the famous Gershwin tune which had been an enormous hit in the 1920s (George

Gershwin and Minnelli had been close friends before the songwriter's premature death from a brain tumour at 39 in 1937) and May after Vincente's mother. The christening at a Hollywood church was a major media event — the studio made sure of that — and gave Liza her first if unknowing experience of being in the spotlight. Judy's close friend Kay Thompson, one-time cabaret artist and writer, was her godmother; her husband Bill Spier was Liza's godfather.

Liza was a healthy and attractive baby and according to her most flattering admirers was to inherit the best features of both her parents. As she developed it was clear that the large brown eyes and full lips would be unmistakably Minnelli, the snub upturned nose and overall looks pure Garland. But psychologically Judy was woefully unprepared for motherhood and though anxious to be caring and dutiful, had little defence against grim periods of post-natal depression. Two months' agreed leave from the studio following the birth seemed to make little difference and Judy continued to resist the idea of going back to work, even after a couple of weeks' extension, reporting at the studio on the very last day.

The Pirate, released in 1948, gave her a starring role opposite Gene Kelly in a wonderfully inventive and gaudily exuberant MGM picture skilfully directed by Vincente Minnelli. Cole Porter had produced an original score which included the captivating 'Be a Clown' and, with Gene Kelly probably approaching the peak of his career, the picture had all the makings of being a major box-office hit. But in the making it was something of an unnerving, chaotic experience. The old tensions of being before the camera — in what was a demanding role for Judy: she portrayed an adult for the first time in a decade of making movies — came flooding back. She had lost much weight and the vulnerability of her physical state, probably still undermined by the trauma of the Caesarian birth, was also disturbing. She couldn't sleep at night, arrived late on the set, and sometimes didn't show up at all. She once again resorted to taking pills which brought on disturbing extremes of mood from intense, depression to near-hysteria.

It was hard for studio executives, the crew and cast to be understanding as Judy's behaviour worsened. She and Vincente quarrelled on the set — not in itself unusual for a director and star, of course — and she accused him of pandering to the star status of Kelly against her own interests. There was also friction because she felt Vincente was often too ready to take the studio's point of view against her. Judy was reputedly being paid $1000 a day, yet would stay away for days on end and finally had to absent herself for regular visits to her psychiatrist. Shooting the film inevitably ran excessively over schedule, but even with the picture finally completed, Judy's condition showed little improvement. In the end, physically spent and mentally unresisting, she entered a private sanatorium close to Los Angeles. The decision was inevitable and ended a period of high emotional tension and drama not only at the studio but at the family home, where the marriage was already stormy.

The hostility and bitterness which had been developing between Vincente and

Judy because of Judy's unstable condition were largely shielded from Liza, who spent much of her time in the care of a dedicated child nurse. Often she would be well protected from her parents' quarrels, being looked after in her own part of the house; and at first she was too young to know. Judy and Vincente would be on their best behaviour during the times they spent with her, being loving and affectionate, and would always make a point of saying goodnight to her.

So it is doubtful if Liza, as a baby and early toddler, would have been affected by her parents' deteriorating relationship. There was never any doubt that both her parents loved her dearly and in their hearts were always impeccably intentioned. Playing the responsible mother Judy would insist on treating Liza from an early age as much like an adult as possible. 'I was always treated like a grown up,' Liza would reveal many years later, explaining that there was never any baby talk because her mother had told her that she felt that there would be plenty of people who would double-talk her when she got older.

Despite the underlying hostility between her parents, the days passed normally for baby Liza. She could crawl rapidly, skilfully negotiating the stairs, at a little over twelve months. She swam when she was two and by all accounts was an adorable infant with those large brown eyes, a bright round face and a fast-developing independent spirit. She soon became used to her mother singing to her and responded with snippets of tunes almost as soon as she could talk. Judy cherished her, but was plagued by feelings of inadequacy and insecurity. Her violent swings of mood made her fearful of what tragedy could occur if her condition was left untreated. It was this fear which led to Judy's agreement to enter a sanatorium for specialized treatment.

Both Vincente and Judy were at first unsure whether to tell Liza that her mother would be going away for a while. She would probably have been too young anyway for it to have registered much with her, but Judy and Vincente agreed, after consultation with Liza's nurse, that she should be told; but not the reasons for Judy's absence. Vincente dutifully took Liza into his arms and told her quietly and sympathetically that mummy had to go away for a while. Liza would soon become used to this sad scenario of often unexpected partings, and consequent reunions, whether through Judy's recurring illnesses or her long hours spent at the studio. Always at these times Judy would miss having Liza around and on that first occasion, while Judy was away having treatment to wean her off her drug addiction, she became desperate to see Liza and asked if she could receive a visit from her. The medics felt that having her daughter with her might be good therapy for Judy and agreed. Taken there by Vincente, Liza was left to toddle into her mother's room unaided and fell into her arms. They cuddled and kissed enthusiastically. Liza was not yet two years old.

It is hardly surprising that Judy's emotional problems had a devastating effect on her marriage. Vincente was by nature restrained, controlled and undemonstrative, forgiving and conciliatory, and for a while some of the rifts which were already showing by the time

Liza was born seemed to be relieved by her arrival. For an interlude Judy and Vincente shared the most joyful time of their lives together. Both adored Liza, but the domestic turmoil which would blight and ultimately destroy their marriage provided no sensible or stable base for parenthood. Judy's feelings of inadequacy and insecurity grew. She contemplated her own childhood and the unhappy relationship she had endured with her own mother, Ethel, and wanted desperately to do better for Liza. Yet she continued to agonize over the possibility that she might fail. She would begin to resent the attention Liza received and increasingly became strained and emotionally stressed. Soon the love which Vincente and Judy had felt for each other (though some time later Judy would say that she had never really loved him), was turned towards Liza, often swamping and confusing her.

But there was need for Judy to work again. *Easter Parade* was a way out of the mounting financial problems which were developing. Despite all their previous difficulties MGM cast Judy with the immaculate Fred Astaire in what was to be a delectable and highly successful movie. Fred had been out of films for a couple of years and was contemplating long-term retirement, but was persuaded to make a swift come-back when Gene Kelly, originally cast in the lead, broke an ankle. Vincente had been chosen to direct the picture, but MGM had second thoughts after talking to Judy's psychiatrist, who considered it unwise for them to work together because of their deteriorating personal relationship. Charles Walters took over as director and Judy worked well on the film, causing little trouble and only occasionally turning up late. She shared three dance routines with Astaire in what would be one of his all-time great movies, showcasing an incredible musical score by Irving Berlin. Fred and Judy's song-and-dance routine in the tramp number, 'We're a Couple of Swells', raced straight into film musical history.

Not slow to detect the enormous commercial value in a re-teaming of the high-voltage Garland with the legendary Astaire, producer Arthur Freed had lined up *The Barkleys of Broadway* before shooting on *Easter Parade* was completed, but even the temptation to work once more with Astaire was not enough to replenish the despairing Judy. Her condition during *Parade* had caused some concern, and never had she shown herself likely to be fit enough to face an immediate follow-up film.

All the old symptoms were back. She couldn't sleep and, at other times, couldn't keep awake. She would become disoriented, unable to know or remember what she was doing. She condemned the studio for pushing her so hard and insisting she keep her youthful image, though by now she was almost twenty-six. She dieted, lost weight, had persistent headaches and, when the time came, was in no condition to start filming. The studio delayed the start but then suspended her. In the end Ginger Rogers was called in to take over from Judy in the final teaming of the famous Astaire-Rogers partnership.

It was all too much for Judy and her marriage. She and Vincente were soon to be man and wife in name only as

Judy moved out into a rented place of her own. For Liza, this troubled home environment meant she would spend more time with her nurse, but never in later years would she give a despairing view of her childhood. Toddlers are often surprisingly independent and resilient, especially if under the almost constant care of a nanny; and, for a baby born of stars in the fairy-tale world of Hollywood, the growing-up process would always provide more than is usual elsewhere in interest and excitement.

When Judy had been making *The Pirate* in 1947 at MGM, with Vincente directing, she had taken the 14-months-old Liza on to the set where she was due to make her fleeting debut in films as a babe in arms held by her mother. She was the centre of attention at the studio as she had her costumes fitted and was photographed with her mother and father. But in the end the film became such a shambles in the making, largely because of Judy's condition, that Liza's anticipated debut did not materialize. But she became a mini-star in her own right, being photographed sitting confidently in her mother's chair on the set. Gazing into a camera lens, as she would do as a 7-year-old on the set of *Lovely to Look At*, became a natural way of life.

It was Judy's twenty-eighth picture, titled *In the Good Old Summertime*, which went out on general release in 1949, that marked Liza's screen debut. She was not quite three years old when the picture was being shot. The ending had Judy and Van Johnson, her co-star, as a married couple walking in the park with their young daughter. Liza is actually billed in the cast list as 'Liza Minnelli (Veronica and Andrew's daughter)' — Veronica and Andrew were Garland's and Johnson's characters in the film. At one point the action called for Johnson to lift Liza high in his arms. The independent Liza had insisted on dressing herself for the part in a white frilly dress but surprisingly had appeared ill at ease during the shooting. It was left to Liza herself to later reveal the source of her anxiety: she had forgotten to put on her panties under her dress.

Liza loved being in front of the cameras and in her early years would relish the times she was able to visit the film studios and mix with the stars. Her mother and father were famous around the film sets and thus allowed special privileges where Liza was concerned. She recounts with cherished delight how she was taken to the studio where her father would allow her to ride on the camera boom. She saw Fred Astaire and Cyd Charisse. Both were particular favourites because as a toddler Liza liked to dance around and would soon begin to show some natural talent for balance and movement. On the set bright sequences and musical numbers particularly attracted her and she said later that as a child all she wanted was to grow up able to dance like Cyd Charisse. In the longer term she would also dwell on the positive side of her talented lineage, saying that she derived her strength, magic and humour from her mother. 'Her humour was so immense, people don't realize that,' she explained in 1991. 'And she gave me my drive. My father gave me my dreams.'

But Judy and Vincente lived the sort of life which at best would have made it hard to bring up their daughter in a normal way. It was an extraordinary life for an infant, even by Hollywood standards. Their fragmented relationship, along with Garland's emotional instability and Minnelli's compensating over-indulgence of his daughter, brought many powerful dramas into Liza's young life. It was to be a life governed by excesses, turmoil, partings and reunions, rows and reconciliations. The love for their daughter, which they each demonstrated spontaneously and in abundance in their more rational moments, was not sufficient compensation, and not always administered with sensible understanding. And how could they make it up to a daughter who was in the same house when, in an extravagant emotion-charged gesture following an argument with Vincente, Judy cut her wrists in a mock suicide attempt? Judy's sense of guilt and shame afterwards when more rational must have made her inconsolable.

Liza would become used to her mother going away for periods, but was ill-prepared for the time when her father, unexpectedly, left her too. Judy was in need of treatment and had been booked into a hospital at Boston. Vincente and Liza went to the train station to see her off. Once there, Judy became so distressed and hysterical that Vincente decided he would have to accompany her to Boston. Though only two months past her third birthday, Liza was old enough to fear the worst. As she tried to hang on to her parents, she was dragged away to be taken home alone with her nanny in the chauffeur-driven car. Years later an adult Liza Minnelli would tell *Good Housekeeping*'s Muriel Davidson: 'I sobbed and screamed to be taken too, but all I could do was stand there and watch the train pull away.' It revealed much about her early years when she added: 'It was my first horrendous recollection.' Vincente was away for three days on that occasion and Judy did not return home for twelve weeks.

After a while even the deep love and genuine affection they had for Liza, and which had kept Judy and Vincente together, was not enough to prevent the inevitable. By the time *In the Good Old Summertime* was filmed they had gone through two trial separations, and it wouldn't be long before Vincente would declare publicly: 'We are happier apart.' For two years, while Judy lived separately with Liza, there would be unsuccessful attempts at a permanent reconciliation. It didn't help when Judy was unable to grasp a major screen opportunity and had to be replaced in the lead role of Annie Oakley in the screen version of *Annie Get Your Gun*. MGM had bought the screen rights to Irving Berlin's Broadway smash hit specifically as a Garland vehicle, at what was reputed to be a record fee for the studio. But sadly once again she was in no condition, either physically or psychologically, to take on such a major, demanding role. She desperately wanted the part, but couldn't find the purpose, energy or direction; and her voice was faltering. She had previously found it difficult to work under the autocratic direction of Busby Berkeley, whom the studio had hired to direct the picture, but not wishing to cause problems had kept her objections to herself. By the time he was fired, to make room for Charles Walters, Judy's system was so conditioned by the drugs she had been taking to tolerate the situation that she was unable to control her movements, and the early scenes were distressing and alarming. Judy was herself mortified when she saw her pitiful performance. Three weeks later she was summarily dismissed from the picture. It meant a token opportunity lost for Liza too, for her mother had announced proudly to everyone within earshot that Liza would be taking the part of one of the children in the film.

It is impossible to say just how the turbulent, bewildering, unpleasant, dramatic, at times euphoric and often chaotic lifestyle of her parents affected the young Liza. But what can be said is that somehow, in spite of everything, there would be episodes of intense joy as colourful, satisfying, enjoyable and brilliant as Judy's own mythical rainbow. One such delightful interval came, unusually, while Judy was completing her treatment at the Peter Bent Brigham Hospital in Boston, and Liza was taken as a three-year-old the three thousand miles from home to stay with her mother. Their weeks together were idyllic. They were together most of the time, sightseeing, meeting people, having their pictures taken, going for walks and having fun on amusement park rides. They talked and hugged one another and played games. During this interlude Judy seemed genuinely more contented, relaxed and happy than for many a day past. She would declare openly her love for Liza and, more confidentially, how she would make every effort in the future to be a better and more caring mother. It was a time for Liza to get to know her mother all over again.

In contrast Vincente had always been a more stable parent, caring and proud, if lacking in some of the finer points of the role. He was often over-protective, not surprisingly, perhaps, in view of Judy's condition, and undemonstrative by nature. Curiously awkward at times in such a personal relationship, he wasn't moved to talk and chatter with his daughter as an on-form Judy would, and approached with some awkwardness the rough and tumble of domestic life. Nonetheless, his heart was in the right place and, particularly because of his feelings for Liza, he tried hard for a time to keep his marriage to Judy intact.

For a while after Judy returned from Boston, she and Vincente enjoyed a welcome renewal of the close relationship which had not existed since Liza had been born. Judy was much improved in mind, body and spirit. She was also more relaxed, and content to be a mother, though perhaps not fully a wife, as much later she was to hint that there had been no sex in her marriage since Liza had been born. But when MGM scheduled a return to work after only three months, wanting her to start on a new picture in November 1949, Judy was once more on the all too familiar treadmill. She had looked forward to working with Gene Kelly again on the picture, to be named *Summer Stock*, but tragically, and perhaps unnecessarily as it turned out, she was instructed to lose weight quickly for the part. The slimming pills brought her weight down, but led to more pills to pep her up, to calm her down, to help her face the responsibilities and stress of film-making. But somehow, miraculously, the picture was completed and scored healthily at the box office.

She was desperately in need of rest, but MGM called her back almost immediately when June Allyson became pregnant after shooting some early footage on a new picture co-starring Fred Astaire called *Royal Wedding* (retitled *Wedding Bells* in Britain). Judy couldn't cope. She wasn't well, began turning up late and would absent herself without warning. Reluctantly MGM sent her a telegram dismissing her from the picture. They replaced her with Jane Powell.

It would prove to be the end of the line for Judy with MGM. Just a few days before Christmas, and on the verge of a mental breakdown, she kissed Liza goodbye and took off for a holiday in New York, but it failed as therapy for the distraught Judy. Liza was at the train station to welcome her home, and the press recorded the happy reunion as Judy hugged her 4-year-old daughter and cried emotionally, 'I love you.' Within days she announced her break from MGM after fourteen years and twenty-eight films and was soon on her way back to New York, where she had acquired an apartment.

Her break from MGM was also to signal a final and irrevocable break from Vincente, who had already moved out of the family home and would remain in California.

Summer Stock, Judy's last film for MGM, was released in 1950 and it was late that year, when Liza was just four years and nine months old, that Judy brought her marriage to an official end by instigating divorce proceedings alleging mental cruelty. In the settlement which followed, Judy retained custody of Liza though Vincente would have equal access to the child.

There is no doubt that in many ways young Liza had a privileged upbringing. She never wanted for food, was always well-dressed and received every attention. She slept safely, was warm and comfortable, had a pretty nursery and paid-for retainers who cared for and looked after her. There was never a shortage of toys and the pampered environment of her Hollywood home provided every material comfort.

But whether she realized it or not, all this was fertile ground for an unnatural and unstable life for Liza, even by Hollywood standards. Judy's violent swings of mood meant that when she was on a high she would overwhelm her child with excesses of attention and love; when the marriage was bumping along at rock bottom Vincente would step in to try to make it up to Liza, but his attention, though less demonstrative, was still oppressive. Nor was he able always to give as much time as he might have wanted, being well committed at the studios.

Liza's early birthdays were celebrated with large, extravagant parties when she and the youngsters of other famous stars were the focus of attention. On such occasions Liza ruled supreme. There would be party entertainers from magicians to trained dog acts and inevitably the programme would include film shows. She was part of a fantasy world in which Liza would not be the only kid to be spoilt and over-indulged. Sometimes she was smothered by all the attention she received; at other times, and in terms of parental presence and attention, she was cruelly neglected.

It isn't surprising that along with a developing independence Liza grew to crave attention and would fight hard for what she wanted, determined to have her own way. Though one fancies that a touch of basic parental discipline might not have gone amiss, Liza would later claim that her mother was a strict disciplinarian — but as with the rest of her life, Judy could swing unpredictably from one extreme to another. All this was in fierce and unfair contrast to Liza's feelings of desertion when her mother was suddenly away ill or spent long days at the studio.

Much later in life she would say that ultimately the only way to get rid of something is to talk about it . . . and to the right person, preferably a pro. Whether Liza sought such a cathartic experience as an adult before she entered the Betty Ford Clinic in 1984 is not certain, but whatever the explanation, she has never herself concentrated too much on the early years of her life. There has never been any suggestion that she was physically abused, and who can say that what she overhead or experienced she did not consider to be the norm. After all, she was cocooned in a Hollywood whose basic environment was anything but that which is generally accepted as normal; though how could Liza at three or four know there was a different world out there? Meantime, her own little life bordered by her nurse and her own room was perhaps a stable, reliable and welcome haven.

What is clear, however, is her intense delight at visiting the film studios where she became known as Princess Liza, and mixing with the kids of other stars. The excitement which later in life she said was a memorable part of her childhood revolved around this unreal world in which international stars like Lauren Bacall, Frank Sinatra, Gregory Peck, Kirk Douglas, Lucille Ball and Sammy Davis Jnr were to her simply 'aunts' and 'uncles'. David Niven was a family friend. She knew Marilyn Monroe and Humphrey Bogart like normal kids know people down the street. When she was twelve she was photographed dancing with Tony Curtis at a party to celebrate Judy's appearance at the

Coconut Grove in Los Angeles. When Mama had guests into the house she was allowed to stay up late. It was a natural part of growing up to play with other children like Mia Farrow, whose mother was Maureen O'Sullivan, and Candice Bergen, daughter of famous ventriloquist Edgar Bergen. Even their real lives were blurred by the candyfloss, make-believe of Hollywood. Fantasy became a normal part of life. Years later Liza would recall playing in the park in Beverly Hills with Mia Farrow, 'Cindy' Bergen, Tish Stirling and others. 'While we were sitting playing we could hear our English nannies talking about picture deals and costume direction and whose employer was going to win an Academy Award,' she explained.

Performing came naturally to Liza. She loved and responded to music at an early age, picking up songs quickly. She was never shy and never hesitated when given the chance to perform. Her godmother, Kay Thompson, recalled for *Time* magazine: 'The language of the house was "What time is rehearsal? When is the next recording session? The script

51

has to be ready for tomorrow." And it was all mixed up with a great rushing to get to the studio.'

There were occasional adventures which brought an almost ecstatic excitement, like in 1951 when she was five and living with Vincente, and Garland, who was touring England, asked if Liza could be sent over to join her. Accompanied by her governess, Liza travelled over on the *Queen Elizabeth* and for about a week was able to stay with her mother in the UK and watch her perform in the theatre from the wings. There were a number of opportunities for Liza to spend time in England with her mother and on one later occasion, when Judy was with Sidney Luft, they moved on to France where mother and daughter spent a happy time swimming off the exclusive beach of the Carlton Club away from the snoopings of the press and public.

After her divorce from Vincente, Judy came to rely increasingly on Liza for comfort and companionship. Judy would confide in her daughter, who as early as three years old would silently listen to stories about difficulties at the studio and how lacking in understanding people at MGM could be. Judy was concerned to treat Liza as honestly and frankly as she could and was constantly on her guard to protect her from the kind of troubled childhood she had experienced with her own mother.

Judy had been born Frances Gumm on 10 June 1922. Her parents, Frank and Ethel Gumm, had been in vaudeville before Frank tried for a more settled existence as the owner of a small cinema in California. Ethel still hankered after the celebrity life and, perhaps trying to fulfil her own thwarted ambitions through her offspring, formed Judy's two older sisters into an act which appeared in the vaudeville part of the cinema programmes of the day. To help supplement the income from the cinema the whole family worked on the stage. Frank and Ethel were billed as Frank and Virginia Lee and the daughters as the Gumm Sisters.

Judy made her stage debut at two and a half and was singing solo at the famous Loews State Theatre in Los Angeles by the time she was six. Screen actress

Dorothy Lamour remembers the time she was on her way to Hollywood by train to begin her own screen career and went to have lunch in the dining car. The man seated opposite told Dorothy that he was also on his way to Hollywood with a song-and-dance act called The Gumm Sisters, one of whom had just been signed to a contract with MGM. Said Dorothy: 'I met the three young girls later in the day. The one who was MGM bound was wearing a sailor dress and looked very cute. About a year later, I went to the Trocadero nightclub for one of their celebrity nights. Lo and behold, that cute little Miss Gumm on the train had changed her name to Judy Garland and was knocking out the audience with her talent — MGM had sent her to their school to groom her for what was to become one of the most brilliant, albeit tragic, careers in the history of Hollywood.'

Judy's mother was a determined and ambitious woman and fought hard to get her children into the movies. Young Judy had the talent and Ethel resolved that her daughter would become a Hollywood star, whether she wanted to or not, though there is no evidence to suggest that Judy wished otherwise. She probably thought it the most natural thing for her to do.

It was this experience with its often painful memories which made Judy nervous, hesitant and protective about young Liza's future, particularly when Ethel began taking Liza to dancing lessons at a local studio. Liza enjoyed this and adored the outings with 'nanna Ethel', but Judy became jealous, suspicious that Ethel, in the way she had manipulated her daughter's life, was now attempting to do the same thing with her grand-daughter. In any event Judy and Ethel were at battle stations for much of Judy's adult life, the friction developing from the time, even before their move to California, when her parents' marriage was no longer meaningful. Judy loved her father and was devastated at the insinuations, and later accusations (generally considered to be true) about his homosexuality.

But despite Judy's misgivings about Ethel's motives, Liza loved dancing from an early age, and also said she would like to be an ice-skater. The dance studio she attended was run under the title of Nico Charisse, who was the former husband of Hollywood dance star Cyd Charisse. Liza's early performance as a 4-year-old in the studio's ballet recital in 1950 was 'splashed' by *Photoplay* magazine with photographs of her in powder puff skirts 'absorbed in a whirl of her own'. The story also revealed Liza's ambition: she wanted to be a ballerina and she also liked the idea of performing, though at this stage acting as such held little attraction for her.

It probably wasn't helped when, only five years old, she took the part of the Virgin Mary in a school Christmas pageant and, with her proud parents in the audience, she embarrassingly dropped the doll she was holding which represented the baby Jesus. Liza's acerbic comment made the rounds for some time. 'I dropped the kid,' she proclaimed. Both parents were impressed with Liza's performance and, whether or not she would admit it, Judy was for the first time given a clear signal that her daughter might follow her as an entertainer.

It was also when she was five that Liza first met Sammy Davis Jnr and saw him perform. Such was Sammy's impact on the impressionable youngster that more than forty years later she recalled: 'I remember very clearly what he did and what he looked like, but most of all I remembered his energy. I couldn't believe how one man could be so great.' It was probably that one particular moment, more than any other, which rooted Liza Minnelli firmly and for life into a musical genre which had been virtually left behind by the time her own generation was topping the bill, making the charts and starring on television.

3

'The Best Lessons are the Most Painful'

LIZA'S parents were divorced on 3 March 1952 when she was just nine days short of her sixth birthday. She had already seen a good deal more of life than most 6-year-olds and the irrevocable severing of matrimonial links would not alter that to any degree. In the eighteen months or so since Judy and Vincente had been separated, Liza had been living with her mother, but would often see her father, spending periods with him and taking unceasing delight in going to the film studios to see him work.

These 'periods of access' with her father were predictable, largely calm and stable. Vincente's talent as a movie director was by now well recognized in the business and, in movies like *The Long, Long Trailer* in 1954 and *Some Came*

Running in 1958, he would prove his creative abilities in drama and comedy, though it was through a variety of truly magical film musicals that he would become best remembered. Liza would recall with delight years later the time she visited the set of *The Long, Long Trailer*, which starred Lucille Ball and Desi Arnaz, and the ecstasy of seeing Gene Kelly and Leslie Caron dancing on the set of *An American in Paris*. Her passion for dancing was underscored by a natural ability and an enthusiastic readiness to perform. Now, without her mother's often bewildering and disturbing presence, she could gather her young friends together and organize a mini musical show within the comfort and security of Vincente's home. A flavour of the real thing was procured through the carefully made replicas of gowns, dresses and other outfits used in recent movies which her father had arranged to have made specially for her, and from his impressive collection of props which included items like hats, canes, shoes, coats and even fake guns.

Time spent with Judy tended to be

more erratic, emotional and disjointed. But it was often also exciting, for when she was feeling well Judy could be affectionate and attentive. There was never any suggestion that Liza blamed her mother or her father for the break-up of the family.

For some time Liza was unaware of the new man who was growing in importance in her mother's life. Garland and Sidney Luft had first met briefly some ten years before, but their relationship developed after meeting again much more recently at a showbiz party in New York given by Jackie Gleason. A tough, muscular man with an active interest in physique training, Luft had a streetwise, chequered history to match. At twelve he had brushed with the police for carrying a revolver; there was a spell in the Royal Canadian Air Force; and for a time he was a test pilot for the Douglas Aircraft Company. Luft clung to the fringes of show business as a fixer, go-between, handler and colourful entrepreneur. The threads of the liaison were strongly woven even before Judy's final split with Vincente, and after her break with MGM it didn't take long for the affair to flourish.

With Judy's film career in tatters it was Luft, the smart opportunist, who saw the possibilities of Judy doing a live concert tour of Britain. He was perceptive enough to know that Garland's style in belting out a song, and her exciting stage presence, could be at their most telling before live audiences. And it was Luft, the expert fixer, who had cleverly managed to negotiate Judy's recent lucrative tour of Britain. Liza's first meeting with the man who would become her step-father was in England when Judy had asked Vincente to send their daughter over.

Judy made her debut at the famous London Palladium and completed a tour of the major provincial theatres. The Brits still loved Judy and the tour was a sell-out success. In the early days Luft was good for Judy. He was clever and adept at handling her career. Bolstered by her British success she was off the pills, feeling and looking good. There was no immediate chance of marriage. Luft's divorce from actress Lynn Bari was not yet final and at this point Judy was still technically married to Vincente. Buffeted about in a kind of emotional no-man's-land between her mother and father, Liza would manage to survive a difficult childhood remarkably unscathed. She became a seasoned traveller early in life.

While Liza spent time with Vincente in California, her mother's successful rebirth as a live performer continued. Luft negotiated a sensational engagement at the famous Palace theatre in New York. Her opening there was the biggest event on Broadway for years. Singing and dancing, recapturing scenes from some of her most famous movies and stepping out with style and infectious enthusiasm, Judy shone with a brilliance which was bewitching and, for her many thousands of fans, deliriously satisfying. Despite a heavy rehearsal programme, and in spite of the three thousand miles which currently separated them, Judy managed to see Liza once or twice. There is no doubt that these meetings were considered precious interludes for both of them.

But, sadly, with Judy the pendulum

could swing to such extremes that Liza might dominate her thoughts at one moment, yet be literally forgotten the next; and often when it mattered most. Judy was at the Palace for more than four months, creating a record for the theatre, but her schedule had to be cut down from thirteen shows a week to ten after she collapsed in the middle of a performance from nervous exhaustion and the effects of dieting. She was away for several nights. Later, battling to control her weight and to keep off the pills and booze, she took a few more days off so that she could spend time with Liza, being the devoted mother and desperate to be close and affectionate.

Yet when the curtain dropped on her final performance at the Palace, she left with Luft for a vacation in Palm Beach and missed Liza's spectacular sixth birthday party at Vincente's home in California. It probably wasn't the first time that Judy had missed an important date in her daughter's calendar; nor would it be the last. But at six years old it might have been difficult for Liza to understand why her mother was not there when she blew out the candles, had it not been that she was by now well accustomed to her mother moving into and out of her life with little or no warning.

Not long afterwards, when the two of them were spending time together, Judy asked Liza what she would think if she were to marry Sid Luft. The youngster wasn't altogether happy with the idea, wondering what would happen to daddy and whether she would be able to see her father if her mother married again. But her eyes brightened when Judy explained that it might mean that Liza could perhaps have a baby brother or sister if she and Sid married; and she began to get excited about the possibility of going to the wedding. Judy knew at the time that she was pregnant and she and Luft had already decided to marry.

But when Judy married Sidney Luft in June 1952 Liza was not invited or even told in advance. It was left to the 6-year-old to hear about it from watching the evening news on television with her father. They had married at a private ceremony in San Francisco. Liza wept, but later rationalized: 'I guess it wasn't my business when Mama got married or to whom.' Judy told her daughter that she had intended telling her about the wedding, but news reporter Louella Parsons had got her story out quicker than she had expected.

The emotional turmoil of her mother's life was to be central to Liza's existence as she grew into a teenager and began to sort out her own destiny. Judy continued to have custody of her daughter and later, as Luft successfully reshaped and rebuilt her mother's fragile career, Liza would be hauled around the country, and was sometimes taken abroad as Judy travelled to a series of theatre and concert engagements. For Judy it helped to foster the 'happy family' scenario she liked to indulge in, but it was more likely to do with the strength and security which Judy gained from having Liza with her.

The nomadic life provided Liza with little chance of gaining a coherent or stable education or of making long-term friends with boys and girls her own age. Precocious and instinctively prone to exaggeration, Liza would claim later in life that she attended some twenty different schools. More likely it was no more than twelve, but certainly more than enough to hamper a creative, progressive education and adolescence. In the end she would go to a variety of schools in California, New York, London and Switzerland as well as spending time at the Sorbonne in France. She learned to speak French and would advance her education to a commendable level while living in London.

For a while, though, Judy's latest marriage brought a degree of stability to Liza's life. They moved into a sumptuous house in one of Hollywood's most privileged areas and, perhaps for the first time in her life, Liza began to feel she was part of a family, for Luft's son Johnny from his previous marriage, some eighteen months younger than Liza, lived with them. It was even better when Judy's second daughter was born, on 21 November 1952, to be called Lorna. Liza, going on seven when Lorna arrived, loved the idea of having a baby sister and at this point was doing well at the exclusive private school she attended daily.

But sadly there was to be for Liza a growing feeling of being left outside the togetherness of the Luft family, particularly as she was sometimes sent off to visit her father when the rest of the family went on visits together. The compensation for Liza was her devotion to her father and the enjoyment of staying with him at his home. She could recapture all the excitement and thrills of the picture-making business as she accompanied him to the studios. The back lot and sound studios became territory as familiar as her own backyard.

Judy's marriage to Sidney Luft would last for thirteen long years and was destined to survive a number of trial separations and countless human dramas. The enmity which grew between them would in the long term play its part in ending her career, along with drink and drugs, and leaving her penniless with mountainous debts. Some of these dramas would touch Liza personally more than others, but seldom would it be possible for her to be completely protected from the influence of highly emotional, sometimes traumatic, even potentially dangerous situations.

Judy's relationship with her mother Ethel, never deeply loving nor strong, even before her marriage to Vincente, had declined over the years and Judy had seldom seen her sisters. Yet she was overcome with grief and guilt when Sid broke the news that Ethel had been found dead between two cars in the parking area of the Douglas Aircraft company. She had apparently suffered a heart attack as she arrived for her work there. It was a devastating moment for Judy, whose lengthy estrangement from her mother had resulted in such a mutual lack of respect and understanding that stories appeared in the press about Ethel having to work on a routine job at Douglas for just a few dollars a day while her famous daughter lived out a life of extravagance and luxury. It was also reported that Ethel had tried to obtain financial support from her daughter, an approach which had been unceremoniously repelled by Judy. A bitter and public lawsuit followed.

So bad had their relationship become that when Lorna had been born it was alleged that Judy told the hospital staff not to let her mother in to see the baby. The unfairness of all this was that Judy, by this time, was apparently making a regular allowance to her mother.

Now, with her mother's death, Judy found it hard to come to terms with herself. Whatever had gone on before, deep down she would not have wished her mother to die without there being some kind of reconciliation, however dutiful. But now, no matter the extent of sorrow or regret, it was all too late. It was just another cross which the tortured Judy would have to bear in her remaining years. She once more sank into an inconsolable state of depression and tried to find a way through it by resorting to pills and liquor and cutting herself off from her children.

It was a familiar scenario for Liza. Sometimes Judy's demoralization was self-induced, as in the case of her reaction to her mother's death, but at other times it was sparked off by natural, if inevitable, causes outside her control. As when Liza had been born, Judy had found little to enjoy when Lorna was on the way. She gained weight excessively, found it difficult to move around, looked gross and was feeling unwell for much of the time. This was followed by another grim period of post-natal depression, which came to a climax when she attempted suicide by cutting her throat, though she later claimed that she could not recall doing it. It was left to Sid to find her slumped on the bathroom floor and to administer crucial first aid. The butler had raised the alarm, telephoning Sid after being unable to get a reply from Judy's bedroom. The doctor stitched up the wound on the spot and the incident was hushed up.

Luft had been acting as Judy's manager and general agent since before they were married, and in an attempt to help her over a similar period of depression following the death of her mother, had redoubled his efforts to get her back into films. The result was a remake by Warner Brothers of the 1937 drama, *A Star is Born*, starring Fredric March and Janet Gaynor. It would be the first time

Judy had faced the cameras in more than three years. Whether the prospect was so daunting that she became momentarily unbalanced is not certain but, following a violent argument with Lorna's nurse one night, she stormed out of the house without warning. The nurse was herself so angry that she quit on the spot, packed her bags and left. Sid was away, and only Liza was left to cope the best she could. She woke up the cook, who helped Liza to look after baby Lorna until her mother returned.

Despite the frenetic lifestyle of her mother, the young Liza would seldom be found wanting when the time came. Judy developed the habit of threatening her own life to gain attention, and while these occasions were often seen by others as no more than a call for help, Liza always took them seriously, raising the alarm or summoning help quickly. Liza tolerated Judy's angry and irrational outbursts with a degree of equanimity far beyond her years, and she became used to looking after herself when Judy stormed out of the house in a rage. She would also welcome her mother's remorseful affection when she returned.

There seems little doubt that Judy increasingly depended on Liza for the emotional balance which she so desperately needed in her life. She was a calming influence on Judy, Vincente would say some years later; she acted as a kind of nursemaid, dresser and general aide. This degree of obligation, whether or not Liza saw it as that, must have placed an extraordinary burden on the youngster. Liza would say later that she always had responsibility and never felt really free until she was twenty. She had grown up in a hurry and, as early as three and four years old, would move back and forth frequently between her mother and father.

Seldom, if ever, however, did she seem to bear a grudge. Indeed Liza obviously adored Judy. It was later, when Liza was determined to make her own way in show business, that the real friction became a problem. This was often a direct result of Judy's intense and illogical jealousy of her daughter's ambitions, generally hidden under the pretence of being protective towards her.

A further moment of anguish for Liza was when Judy's third child was born. Joseph Wiley Luft arrived almost two weeks early (Frank Sinatra became his godfather), on 29 March 1955, with a life-threatening lung disorder. It was Liza to whom Judy turned, telephoning her to say the baby was a boy and, distressed, telling her daughter that the doctors had said that he might die. 'But he's not going to die, I promise you,' she asserted. By the following morning the boy was out of danger, but for the 9-year-old Liza it was just one more emotional hazard to cope with.

Another problem for Liza was her increasing sense of isolation. Vincente had married for a second time to Georgette Magnani in February 1954 and his second daughter, Tina Nina, was born just a few weeks before Joseph (Joey) Wiley. More and more, Liza seemed not to belong completely to anyone. The new babies on both sides of the family naturally claimed much of the attention which had previously been focused on Liza. As time went by she must have become increasingly confused, unsettled, resentful, frightened, yet often loving as Judy, under a heavy intake of pills and alcohol, would rage and shut herself away threatening suicide, only later, when all had calmed down, sneaking into Liza's bedroom to crave forgiveness. It brought Liza a sense of maturity long before this was naturally due, but also, and not unnaturally, a tense, nervous disposition which manifested itself in her high-energy, surface-excitability.

Her life continued to be one of extremes and excesses. As Judy began to lose touch with her once lucrative career, Liza would stand by helpless as her mother ran out of confidence, patience, energy, even money. While some would ponder the tragedy of Judy Garland's life, Liza was left to count the personal cost at a more practical level: moving out of a hotel or a rented house under cover of darkness (carrying or wearing as many personal belongings as possible) because Judy couldn't meet the payments; and having to leave her private school for the same reason.

She would explain many years later that her childhood was interesting, though it had nothing to do with being a child. It had much more to do with 'mothering' her mother. She said that as a 6-year-old she knew how to dial room service and could quote Oscar Wilde. At ten years old she was playing the adult, listening to her mother telling her how lonely she was. At eleven she would hire and fire the household staff when her mother felt she couldn't cope with it. At fourteen she would be driving Lorna and Joey to school because, as she would explain, 'our chauffeur was drunk all the time and Mama liked him too much to fire him.' She would take over when Judy forgot to pay the bills and make the right excuses when she missed appointments; not to mention coping with Judy's pill-taking and suicide attempts. There would be horrendous stories of Liza and Lorna tampering with their mother's pill supplies, trying to protect her by secretly replacing some of the offending tablets with others which looked the same but were less harmful. Days were a bizarre mixture of fairy-tale and grim reality.

Of course when Judy did a successful concert tour the money would flow in again and she would regain her confidence, fired with renewed energy and clinging to Liza, over-protective and over-attentive to make up for the bad times. For Liza it was an unconventional childhood to say the least; dominated by apprehension and uncertainty, yet for one so young she seems to have been almost instinctively philosophical about it all. Much later Liza would admit that life with her mother was a constant melodrama of highs and lows, of, as she told writer Michiko Kakutani in 1988: ' . . . painful falls from grace and even more dazzling come-backs. There were no middles, no times when I was just tranquil.' But by the time she was a teenager she became her mother's best friend and confidante and even later in life would display few permanent scars from earlier years, much preferring to comment on the good times she remembered. Perhaps her own vulnerability as an adult would stem as much from an excessively high level of emotion, excitement, tension and drama inherited from her mother, as from any permanent damage resulting from psychological maltreatment as a child. For even as young as eight, Liza seemed to have accepted to a remarkable degree the inevitability of her life.

And it must be said that, in circumstances which were often difficult, Judy tried hard to be an exemplary mother. She would nurse Liza through various illnesses, take an interest in her school work, be concerned with her dates and boyfriends, and even when, as journalist Kakutani also pointed out, 'her sense of being was threatened by a younger version of herself . . . she gave her daughter encouragement and support with advice about singing and acting.'

In 1954, Judy's so-called comeback film, *A Star is Born*, was released. Ultimately, and in comparison with a much later rock version featuring Barbra Streisand and Kris Kristofferson, Judy's film was to gain status and critical acclaim, particularly for its musical content, but at the time the public response was disappointing. Luft had planned the picture to help Judy out of an exceptionally bad spell and, after organising all the finance, he assumed the role of producer, the famous George Cukor taking over as director.

Making the film became a nightmare. Judy often found it hard to concentrate, there were tantrums, she would frequently arrive late and sometimes wouldn't turn up at all. The picture ran grossly over budget. Yet despite these exceptional odds, she managed to turn in an outstanding dramatic as well as musical performance. It was arguably the best work she had ever done and her sensitive portrayal of the unknown singer who becomes a superstar while her husband's one-time star career crashes into excessive booze, bewilderment, disillusionment and finally suicide, put Judy in pole position for an Oscar.

Martin Sutton wrote some years later in *The Movie*: 'Judy Garland was peculiarly right for the role. It is impossible to watch this *A Star is Born* without reflecting on the problems of Garland's own life. And this factor resulted in her most electrifying performance.' Sutton goes on: 'By this stage in her career, no gesture or expression is wasted and she turns the torchy interlude of a song like

'The Man that Got Away' into a small powerhouse of its own.'

Liza visited the Warner Brothers sound stage several times to see her mother working on the picture and was spellbound. It was also in the 1954-released picture *The Long, Long Trailer*, directed by her father and starring Lucille Ball and Desi Arnaz, that she made an unbilled appearance, unaware as an 8-year-old that some years later she would come close to marrying their son. Everything seemed to be working out well for Judy with *A Star is Born*. The premiere was an enormous success and the critics were ecstatic. It was hard to see how she could miss the Best Actress award.

She wanted the accolade very badly, but when the winners were announced Judy's outstanding performance was overlooked and the Oscar went to Grace Kelly for *The Country Girl*. Sid had spent the time waiting for the results with Judy in hospital where she was preparing for the birth of their first son. He was furious about the snub and would never produce another motion picture. Judy was distraught and would not go before the film cameras again for almost six years. It was early the following morning that she gave birth to Joey.

Over the years there would be an enormous volume of speculation about the relationship between Liza and Judy, as commentators and writers probed masses of comment, press reports and documents from all kinds of sources in their search for the truth. Fertile ground indeed for the mystique, which developed with the passing of time, and in the absence of an autobiography from Liza. But one thing is indisputable: it was Judy who first gave Liza the opportunity to express herself in public, an opportunity which, in the end, led to Liza's own career in show business. There was that fleeting glimpse of Liza in *In the Good Old Summertime* in 1949 when she was not quite three years old. It was also Judy who either initiated or condoned her planned, and as it turned out, abortive appearance a year earlier in *The Pirate*, in which Judy starred and Minnelli directed. From her mother Liza drew the courage, and received the encouragement, to perform at home, singing her mother's songs and acting during impromptu shows. She would be grateful to her mother for some of those early visits to the film studios.

When she was almost eleven, and Judy was appearing at the Palace theatre in New York, her mother insisted she be flown over from California to see her perform. At one point in the show she called for Liza and her daughter was lifted up on stage and did a dance while Judy sang 'Swanee'. Judy knew she could do it, having seen her perform many times at home. Never mind that Judy was having difficulty with some of the songs and her action was prompted by the need to divert the audience's attention. For this stage debut Sid Luft presented the wide-eyed, long-haired Liza with a $5 bill which was later framed and hung on her wall. It was in a similar situation and for similar reasons that a year later Judy called her daughter up on stage while appearing in Las Vegas. This time Judy announced a surprised and unrehearsed Liza and then left the stage entirely to her daughter. Liza sang five songs before departing and the patrons thought it was all part of the act. When she was fourteen Liza was taken by her mother to see some Broadway shows and loved the experience. She thought being on stage seemed a lot of fun, with everyone fooling around and having a good time. At fifteen she was on TV with her mother. And of course, there was that momentous occasion a long time later in 1964, at the Palladium, when Judy and Liza shared top of the bill.

She once said that it was also her mother who showed her, through her example, how to survive, adding that you don't acquire wisdom with a smile on your face. 'Usually the best lessons are the most painful,' she said. That is perhaps why she never spoke harshly about her childhood. Repeatedly in the years ahead Liza would concentrate on the happy and positive elements of her life. She told journalist Michiko Kakutani in 1984: 'There is nothing I can say to convince people that I had a happy childhood, they don't want to believe that.' She went on: 'It's your life and there aren't any comparisons. I mean, how do you ask a princess what it's like to be a princess — she doesn't know, it's the only thing she's ever been.'

In her formative years Liza would accept the glitzy, glamour 'little princess' interludes of her life with the mature assurance of the showbiz trouper she was born to become. At six she welcomed her mother back from New York after her Palace Theatre triumph. At eleven she was photographed frolicking with Judy, Lorna, Joey and Johnny Luft in the grounds of their luxurious, filmstar-style Mapleton Drive home. At twelve she was on stage with Judy at the famous Coconut Grove in Los Angeles. At thirteen she was seen dancing with her father at an exciting Hollywood party. And when she was fifteen she was in the audience at Judy's historic return to Carnegie Hall.

For a long time, though, Liza had no serious ambition to be a singer or an actress. As with many young girls, dancing of one sort or another was the basis of her impromptu performances; but despite so much enthusiasm for it as a child, when she prepared for her starring role in the picture, *Stepping Out*, released in 1991, she had to undertake rigorous training in tap to bring her technique up to scratch. She said at the time: 'I lost 15 lb in three weeks and by the time I had finished filming I lost another twelve.'

When the subject of Liza's ambition for a career in entertainment finally came up Judy responded with a typical comment: 'I think she decided to go into show business when she was an embryo, she kicked so much.' But Liza realized that her mother's party joke wasn't much short of the mark, measured against her idea as an infant to become an ice skater, then a dancer, later still a singer, and finally an actress. Never once, it appears, did she gaze at the emotional burden a career in show business had placed on her mother and consider . . . this can't be for me. Though she perhaps did not realize it at the time, she later admitted that she never once thought about doing anything else.

Liza's day of firm decision came while she was studying at the Sorbonne in Paris. Vincente Minnelli explained that she sent a telegram to Judy, who was appearing in Las Vegas, saying that she was coming home and wanted to talk

Born to be a star
and later recognized as one of the world's
most exciting performers.

With Julie Walters in *Stepping Out,* her best picture since *Cabaret.*

Liza knocking her dance class into shape in *Stepping Out.* Director Lewis Gilbert wouldn't have done the movie if Liza couldn't have been cast in the star role.

Captivating audiences with a solo performance at London's Royal Albert Hall in October 1991.

Liza is electrifying with her troupe of dancers during the same 'live' presentation.

With Dudley Moore in a scene from the 1981 picture *Arthur*, which brought Sir John Gielgud an Oscar.

On the set of *Stepping Out* with director Lewis Gilbert.

to her mother. Judy always claimed that she instinctively knew what Liza wanted to talk to her about and, ever the pro, upstaged her daughter. Before Liza could utter a word, Judy blurted out: 'Liza darling, why don't you go into show business?'

The year was 1962. Liza was sixteen. Shortly after, she struck out on her own and went to live in New York. One year later Liza was to make her debut on the New York stage.

4

Youngest-ever Tony
and Almost an Oscar

FOR a time the dichotomy of Liza's professional and private life would continue. When she first set her sights seriously on a career as an entertainer in 1962, her mother's marriage to Sidney Luft was chaotic. There had already been bruising separations and unsteady reconciliations, and the relationship was doomed. It ended in divorce in May 1965, when Liza was still only nineteen. Three and a half years would bring Judy's untimely and tragic death and only then would Liza, twenty-three years old, be able to register her own individual talent and begin to shed the spectre of being Judy Garland's daughter.

Having a famous mother didn't appear to help much at the beginning. It probably opened a few doors, but Liza would find that being so much like Judy was often a drawback. It seemed that agents and others who might have helped her secure a toe-hold in show business could not quite make up their minds. On the one hand they would seem curiously disappointed that she was so much like her mother; yet on the other cynically unsure that what differences there were in looks and manner could be turned to commercial advantage. The crucial point was that she was the daughter of Judy Garland and, in the event, Judy's high-risk profile as an entertainer did not always work to Liza's advantage. As one possible door-opener put it: 'God, that's just what we need — Judy Garland's daughter!'

Judy, despite her claim that she encouraged Liza to go for a professional career in show business — even put the thought into her mind — didn't offer any cash to help get her started. She knew also that show business could lead to failure and heartbreak; and she considered Lorna to possess the greater potential talent of her two daughters. Liza took off, her sights set on Broadway, with no more than $100 in her handbag, booking herself into a small room in the Barbizon Hotel for Women. She had already smashed the frame holding the $5 bill which Sid Luft had given her, to help pay her way to New York. The vital break into show business did not come instantly, the money ran out, and Liza found herself with no place to sleep and much of her luggage confiscated. For a time she camped out in the open and used the hospitality of family contacts, but fortunately a few modelling assignments for teenage magazines enabled her to move into tiny rooms in backstreet hotels. She was also sensible enough to invest some of her meagre resources in drama and voice coaching with good teachers in Greenwich Village. Resolute, she was determined to make it on her own and refused to ask Vincente for help. Ultimately, of course, there was a certain novelty value, even notoriety, in being Judy Garland's daughter. At least it picked Liza out from the crowd of other desperate hopefuls trying to break the hard crust of New York's grim off-Broadway theatreland.

But she did have some experience to

talk about. As far back as the autumn of 1955, when only nine, she had made her first television appearance as one of four school-children interviewed on the daily *Art Linkletter Show*. Linkletter was a family friend. Judy was pregnant at the time and Linkletter asked Liza if she hoped her mother would have a boy or a girl. 'A girl,' she replied without hesitation, 'boys are so messy'. The following year marked her impromptu stage debut when Judy called her up on stage at the Palace Theatre in New York. And in December 1956 she was again seen on TV screens, somewhat awkwardly co-hosting with Bert Lahr the first network telecast of Judy's classic feature, *The Wizard of Oz*, which had first been shown as a movie in 1939. Not until almost two years later was she seen again on national television, in the *Jack Paar Show*. Then, in April 1959, when thirteen, she sang and danced with Gene Kelly to the tune of 'For Me and My Gal'.

The background to this was that Kelly was a friend of both Vincente and Judy and had first heard Liza sing the song informally with others when a few people gathered around the piano at a party given by Lee and Ira Gershwin at their home, Liza going there with her father. Kelly was impressed by Liza and thought it would be an idea to have her sing the song on a television special he was planning. The obvious link was that in 1942 he had made his screen debut in the film *For Me and My Gal*, when his co-star Judy had sung the title song. Vincente and Judy approved Kelly's idea, Liza was delighted and the programme went out on 24 April 1959, less than six weeks after Liza's thirteenth birthday.

James Spada, in *Judy and Liza*, (Sidgwick and Jackson, 1983) says it featured a 'self-possessed Liza wearing a well-tailored suit and a bow in her hair. Kelly gave her an affectionate introduction, telling the story of hearing her sing at the Gershwins'. With Kelly she sang and danced to 'For Me and My Gal' in a little-girl voice highly reminiscent of Judy's. Kelly apparently thought highly of the 13-year-old Liza's abilities. "Her voice makes you think of Judy. She's got the same kind of pathos.

She is sweet and charming with a lot of her mother's qualities . . . she could certainly go professional if she wants to".' The following year she summoned all her courage and sang her mother's song 'Over the Rainbow' on *Hedda Hopper's Showcase* programme on television. But none of this made her into an overnight juvenile star.

As a 14-year-old the 5' 4½" Liza was extremely chubby, weighing almost 11 stone at the time of the Hopper show and, with shortish hair, looking rather plain; however she was sharp and intelligent and still captivated by all forms of dance. Before she was fifteen she had enrolled for formal professional training at New York's famous High School of Performing Arts, which was the inspiration for the smash hit television series, *Fame*. How much she gained from the short time she was at the famous school is unclear, but it did provide the background to her first recorded romance with a fellow student called Bobby Mariano. Liza was certain she was deeply in love and also impressed that Bobby worked after school in the chorus of the

Dick Van Dyke-Chita Rivero musical, *Bye, Bye Birdie*. Another fellow student was Marvin Hamlisch, who became her best friend, but with whom she was never in love. Hamlisch was perhaps even less well-known than Liza at that time, but the two of them were kindred souls. They got together to make a demonstration record of sorts of Liza, in the hope of impressing record companies. Nothing happened. Hamlisch, however, was later to compose her vocal arrangements, as well as helping with the preparations for her first nightclub act and with her early records. More than ten years would elapse before Hamlisch became a big name in 1974 with an Academy Award for the title song from the film, *The Way We Were*, which was followed by *The Sting*. Liza, however, at about this time appeared with other students in the 'Steam Heat' number from *Pyjama Game* in a hospital benefit performance.

She also attended the public high school at Scarsdale, a fashionable suburb of New York City. Judy was living in Scarsdale at the time, and being a daughter of the famous was not calculated to make Liza the most popular student in the school. Some students resented her flashy background. Others were jealous of it, yet at the same time might have tried to enjoy the reflected glory of her friendship. But Liza largely disappointed them all, including the teaching staff, with her almost constant gum-chewing, dishevelled hair and unkempt 'beatnik' appearance. They had expected the daughter of someone as famous as Garland to reflect the glossy Hollywood image and be well groomed and dressed, ultra-glamorous and spotlessly clean with a pride in her appearance. Her bohemian attitude shocked them. Liza didn't really fit in, found it hard to make friends, and generally seemed to be out of tune with the school and the other students.

She said: 'I couldn't find anyone who was as bright as I was. I guess it was because I grew up with adults . . . kids just weren't into adult conversations like philosophy or literature or anything like that. I'd start a conversation and nobody would join in!'

But the attitudes changed when, in September 1961, she scored a personal triumph in the leading role in the school drama club's production of *The Diary of Anne Frank*. Judy, in the audience with Sid Luft, was so moved and impressed by her daughter's performance that she agreed to finance the sending of the entire production on an overseas tour the following summer. In the meantime, during the summer of 1961, Liza had apprenticed herself at the Cape Cod Melody Tent in Hyannis, Mass. The family's rented house was opposite the Kennedy compound and she, along with Lorna and Joey, became friends with the Kennedy children. More significantly, she appeared in the chorus of *Wish You Were Here*, *Flower Drum Song* and *Take Me Along*.

Even this early in her career, Liza would have to get used to being known more as Judy Garland's daughter than for any talent or promise she might possess. Over the following years, whatever reviewers and critics might say about her performances, they never missed pointing up the family connection. It would be a source of increasing irritation and annoyance to Liza, who wanted so much to be judged for herself and not in comparison with her mother or because her mother was Judy Garland. One exception to this, however, was in 1964 when, the family connection emphasized, Liza proudly recorded the voice of Dorothy for a feature cartoon film called *Return to Oz* (also *Journey Back to Oz*). She later regretted doing it and was embarrassed, since it was designed as a crude exploitation of Judy's original picture, *The Wizard of Oz*. All that Liza had to do was mimic her mother's voice and sing a few songs. It didn't see the light of day until the 1970s, and wasn't seen in the UK until 1973, and then only as a minor release.

Yet, despite the extent of Liza's resolve to be her own person, when that all-important early break finally materialized, it was as much because of who she was as for what she could do as a performer. Producer Arthur Whitelaw was putting together an off-Broadway revival of the 1940s Broadway success *Best Foot Forward* and thought, wisely as it turned out, that casting the daughter of show business icon Judy Garland would give his production a box office boost. He sent someone to find Liza to offer her the chance to audition for one of the major parts. That person was a talent scout of Danny Daniels, the show's director and choreographer and the same Danny Daniels who would choreograph her solo, show-stopping routine in *Stepping Out*, released twenty-eight years later in 1991. Liza thought she had blown her big chance when she was twenty minutes late getting there, but her singing of 'The Way You Look Tonight' and 'They Can't Take That Away from Me' was impressive enough. Whitelaw was delighted and offered her a contract, convinced that having Judy Garland's daughter in the cast was an astute move. It would generate useful publicity and might even capture the imagination of some of the major critics, who normally wouldn't be expected to show interest in an off-Broadway production.

At her first dance rehearsal Liza stumbled over an uneven floorboard and broke a bone in her left ankle. She was horrified and thought the disaster might cost her her big chance, but the injury wasn't all that serious though it meant that Liza would spend the following day, her seventeenth birthday, in a hospital bed with her foot immobilized in a plaster cast. She had proudly telephoned her mother to tell her of her success at the audition and Judy, as ever unpredictable, responded enthusiastically. She told her friend Jack Paar the news and suggested he invite Liza on to his TV show, then a major attraction nationwide. 'Make sure everyone gets a good view of your injured foot', Judy instructed Liza. The producers did better than that. In an innocent subterfuge Liza was announced as Dyju Langard (for anyone alert enough to work it out, an anagram of Judy Garland), a new Armenian discovery, and Liza made sure that the cameras focused on her plastered foot. Only after she had finished her song was her true identity revealed. The hoax was an outstanding success. In the end the opening of *Best Foot Forward* was held back three weeks, by which time Liza was almost fully recovered. It is doubtful if any off-Broadway show had benefited from so much preliminary media attention. Even

Liza's injury couldn't have been better located since a damaged foot, unlike an injury to her back or arm, was a perfect link for more excellent news coverage. For wasn't her show called *Best FOOT Forward*?

When the 16-year-old Liza had arrived in New York just a few months earlier she had still weighed in excess of 10 stone, but between March and April she shed almost 20 lb. She looked good and confident when she stepped on stage for the first time. The show opened on 2 April 1963, just a month after Liza's seventeenth birthday, in front of influential critics and reviewers drawn there by all the pre-opening publicity. The impact was such that Lewis Funke in the *New York Times* likened it to an off-Broadway opening which had been transformed into a Broadway premiere; and reviews were generally good, Liza's personal performance receiving excellent notices.

The excessive publicity had brought out such large crowds, hoping for a glimpse of Liza and perhaps Judy, that the police had to put up control barriers. It was more like a full-scale glittering Broadway opening than what it really was: a first-night performance in a shabby, poky theatre which held fewer than 200 people and was built into the back room of a bar on 73rd Street in Manhattan.

But for Liza it might well have been the Winter Garden in New York or the London Palladium. She was contracted to the full run of the show at the Equity minimum of $35 a week — representing security almost beyond belief compared with the breadline existence she had endured when first moving to New York. Sadly, the excitement and exhilaration of that opening night were to be marred for Liza because Judy, who had promised she would be there, didn't show up. There was no message, no call of explanation. Bitterly disappointed and more than a little angry amid her sobs and tears, Liza called her mother at the intermission to find out what had happened. Judy said she thought the opening had been the following night. 'But you knew it was tonight', responded Liza angrily. Sid Luft would later make a statement to the effect that Judy didn't turn up because she didn't want to draw any of the attention away from Liza on her big opening. Judy was there the following night, with Sid, Lorna and Joey, but nothing could make up for Liza's misery at her mother's absence from her important debut. But if Mama had missed the opening, Papa certainly hadn't. He was there to congratulate her. He thought his daughter's performance was wonderful. Said Vincente afterwards: 'I must admit I was more emotionally involved during her performance than I had expected to be.'

Judy might have felt that eventually she would be able to smooth things over with her daughter, but Liza wouldn't easily or quickly forget the incident. She had been very upset and bitterly disappointed. It was a long time before the vision of those empty seats which had been reserved for Judy and Sid on opening night faded from her mind. However, reviews of the show, and particularly Liza's performance, were very good and while there was scarcely one which didn't mention the fact that Liza Minnelli was Judy Garland's daughter, the young Liza was delighted with such comments as ' ... a new star is born ... ' and ' ... a wealth of musical talent ... ' Realistically, *Best Foot Forward* lacked a strong story-line and was somewhat lightweight as a show, but most ticket holders had gone to see Liza, and by the time the show closed on 13 October 1963, after almost a seven-month run, she could feel that she was perhaps at last on her way to a successful professional career in entertainment.

Best Foot Forward might have run longer, but as Liza's role was technically not one of the leads — it was the third lead in fact — the management felt justified in encouraging her to take on other engagements like appearing on television, opening stores, and doing interviews, even if these sometimes conflicted with her performances at the theatre. Liza was the most marketable member of the cast and while these 'moonlight' appearances were undeniably good for the show in publicity terms, Liza's increasing absences from performances angered patrons, most of whom had bought their tickets for the novelty value of seeing Judy Garland's daughter, and after reading her good reviews. It didn't help that the avaricious management refused to give refunds to disgruntled patrons. Even so, the show might still have run longer had it not been for Judy. Perhaps for the first time in her professional career, though by no means the last, Liza was used by a possessive, unreasonable mother who could resort to solicitous guile and deceit to get what she wanted. Despite Judy's recent exceptional efforts to secure television interviews for her daughter by pestering all her media contacts, Judy wanted Liza to come back home to California to be with her.

Liza had wanted to continue the show and, besides, had become fond of a young dancer named Tracy Everitt, who was then making his way in the chorus of *How to Succeed in Business Without Really Trying*. Once she realized that Liza could not be persuaded to join her in Los Angeles, Judy cunningly offered Everitt a dancing job on her important forthcoming television series, *The Judy Garland Show*, put out from Hollywood. It was a big career opportunity for the youngster and more than enough to attract him away from New York. Liza had been convinced that she was desperately in love with Bobby Mariano while at the High School of Performing Arts in New York, but now, at seventeen and a half, she was even more intense about her latest relationship. It is not difficult to understand that, in spite of her own career ambitions, she decided to quit the show to follow Everitt to Hollywood and thus, happily for Judy, ended up close to Mama.

Liza's departure signalled the end of the show. Advance sales fell sharply and Arthur Whitelaw, displeased by Liza's leaving, was later to bemoan: 'The show was a success. It was selling out. We could have run for two years.' Liza's place was taken by Marcia Levant, but not too long before the show closed, Hollywood star Veronica Lake was recruited in a vain attempt to save the show, but by then *Best Foot Forward* had effectively run its course. Within six weeks of Liza's final leaving, the show closed. One comforting and encouraging postscript for Liza was the success of her recording of 'You

Are For Loving'. This attractive song had been specially written for the show and she had recorded it as a single separately from the version in the cast LP album. The single sold close to half a million copies and put her in demand for television and personal appearances. She was also featured on the prestigious *Ed Sullivan Show* around this time.

Despite the circumstances, the reunion with her mother was hugely successful, exciting and loving. Judy was emotionally upbeat at having Liza with her again, and Liza responded, caught up in Judy's enthusiasm and expressions of affection. This was in stark contrast to the periods when they would be antagonistic towards each other, like the time Judy would be given the legal authority by the courts to take control of all Liza's earnings.

Liza was still only seventeen and, it seems, not quite as adept at handling money sensibly as at earning it. She suddenly found that she was $3,000 in debt with no immediate hope of clearing the imbalance. She was determined not to turn to her father or mother for help. Judy was very much involved because of a contract she had signed on behalf of the 'under-aged' Liza, and in trying to sort out the problem the court ordered all Liza's earnings to be turned over to Judy, who was required to deposit them in a bank in Liza's name. Only with the court's permission would Liza be able to take any of her money, a situation which pertained until she was twenty-one in 1967. Furious at the ruling, Liza had asked the court if she could keep and control 50 per cent of her earnings, but the request was turned down. Sensibly Liza had given a lawyer power of attorney and the important issue was that her debts were cleared up, but as she was to remark lightheartedly many years later: 'How about that . . . I was seventeen and bankrupt!'

In the meantime, though, the expensive Judy Garland television shows were being taped for nationwide screening and for the third show, taped in July 1963, Liza was Judy's principal guest, her recent success qualifying her for such a key spot. Judy was tense and on pills in an attempt to keep slim, so was in no frame of mind to respond positively and sensibly when

CBS-TV executives criticized the first two shows. The emotional stress was just too much for Judy when she was required to sing the song 'Liza', with special lyrics written by Mel Torme, while walking through a selection of picture blow-ups of Liza during various stages of her young life. As Torme, who was in control of special material for the series, was later to explain in his book, *The Other Side of the Rainbow*: 'She (Judy) wept openly as she sang . . . looking at the pictures all the while and shaking her head from side to side emotionally. Liza ran up on stage at the finish of the song and embraced her mother tearfully. There was nothing phoney about this overt display of affection. Judy loved her kids actively and passionately and her devotion was returned in kind.'

The series which had held out so much promise for Judy never achieved target ratings against the blockbuster *Bonanza* and was terminated. But her featured appearance with Judy on 17 November 1963 was an important if traumatic development in Liza's career. As James Spada explains in *Judy and Liza*: 'The

"Liza Show" ... turned out as a charming hour, with Judy and Liza playfully duetting on 'Together', 'We Could Make Such Beautiful Music Together', 'Bob White', 'The Best is yet To Come', 'Bye Bye Baby', 'Let Me Entertain You', 'Two Lost Souls' and 'I Will Come Back'.'

In early 1964, Liza returned to New York against her mother's wishes to appear as Lili in a stock production of the successful Broadway musical show, *Carnival*, which led to the angry scenes between mother and daughter already described in chapter 1. Judy was now displaying the difficult side of her Jekyll and Hyde character, and her emotional state showed no improvement after she had departed for Australia accompanied by her latest love interest, Mark Herron, an actor some ten years younger than Judy.

Meantime, while high drama was enacted on the other side of the world, Liza was beginning to make inroads in her own country. In June 1964 she took the title role in the comedy play *Time Out for Ginger* at the Buck's County

Playhouse in New Hope, PA and in the summer of 1965, when Liza was nineteen, she gained useful experience touring the USA and Canada with Elliott Gould in *The Fantasticks*. By this time she had become something of a veteran on the small screen, having appeared on national television in the USA and Britain some two dozen times, and was also about to do her first recordings for Capital.

Liza! Liza!, her first complete LP, was an auspicious debut. It was released in the United States in December 1964, re-issued under the title *Maybe This Time*, and first released in Britain under this later title in 1973. (She had previously featured in the original cast recording of *Best Foot Forward* more than eighteen months earlier, being featured solo on just one song — 'You Are For Loving'.) The twelve tracks included a song which would become forever associated with Liza — 'Maybe This Time', gaining its greatest impetus from being included in *Cabaret*, Liza's first major screen triumph almost eight years later. Also included on this first LP, now something of a collector's item, were 'It's Just a Matter of Time', 'If I Were in Your Shoes', 'Meantime', 'Try to Remember', 'I'm All I've Got', 'Maybe Soon', 'Don't Ever Leave Me', 'Travellin' Time', 'Together Wherever We Go', the old standard 'Blue Moon' and 'If I Knew Him When'. By the end of 1967 the *Liza! Liza!* album had sold half a million copies, which led to Liza signing a new contract with Herb Alpert's AEM Records. With this first LP began Liza's career-long association with the talented song-writing team of Kander and Ebb; two of the songs ('Maybe This Time' and 'If I Were in Your Shoes') were from this prolific team, while 'Travellin' Time' was by her friend Marvin Hamlisch. Her forthcoming concert triumphs would also become successful albums.

It might not have been surprising had Judy shed a tear or two when she first heard Liza singing 'Maybe This Time', for the similarities of their voices was particularly striking on this track. The emotional intensity in the voice, the phrasing, the power (not perhaps the level of Judy's at her most robust), and the, at times, difficult to control theatrical talent, if not Judy's hint of a lisp, were all there to recognize and enjoy. Capital released *It Amazes Me* in America in June 1965 with Liza singing 'Wait Till You See Me', 'My Shining Hour', 'I Like the Likes of You', 'Looking at You', 'I Never Have Seen Snow', 'Plenty of Time', 'For Every Man', 'Lovelei', 'Shouldn't There be Lightning' and 'Nobody Knows Me'.

By this time Liza's romantic interest in the dancer Tracy Everitt had been extinguished and already there were the beginnings of what was to become a lifetime of liaisons, entanglements, love affairs and relationships. Men younger and older than she would capture her affections and not unnaturally many of these men were from her own world of show business. Three times she would marry within thirteen years, the first time to an Australian entertainer called Peter Allen, whom Judy had met while in Hong Kong. Allen and his partner, Chris Bell, had been appearing as the Allen Brothers in cabaret in Australia before moving on to Hong Kong. Judy was so impressed with their act that she decided to hire them as part of her own act and persuaded them to accompany her back to Britain to further their career. There was also the suggestion that she had Peter Allen lined up as a prospective marriage partner for Liza. He was an attractive young man in his early twenties, personable, and talented.

Judy made the necessary introductions in London and it appears they were instantly attracted to one another and became technically engaged within weeks. They would probably have married then had not Vincente stepped in to express his concern that Liza, still not quite nineteen and with a whole career opening up ahead of her, was too young to be distracted with thoughts of marriage. Judy, surprisingly, agreed with Vincente, though her motives were perhaps less clear and reputable, considering her hope that the youngsters might be persuaded to tour with her to bolster her own flagging career. Liza moved in with Peter. They were comfortable and Liza's career was working out well. At one point, while Judy was going through one of her difficult phases, the 16-year-old Lorna and Joey moved out to stay with Liza and Peter for a while.

Meantime Liza's starring role with her mother at the London Palladium in 1964 had boosted her reputation and the day after her engagement she flew to New York to audition for a new show called *Flora, The Red Menace*, to be directed by veteran George Abbott who, with Robert Russell, had co-authored the book on which the Broadway show would be based. She had attended earlier auditions — though Liza was perhaps exaggerating when she said she auditioned four times and won the part at the fifth attempt — making the journey from London where she had been with her mother. But she had made little impression on the resolute Abbott, who was determined not to cast her because he considered her unsuitable and didn't believe she had the stage experience to carry it off.

Of course he had a point. There was little real evidence Liza could point to except *Best Foot Forward*, and there seemed to be no real purpose in the mid-Sixties in casting an unknown in a lead role; only risk. So Liza's off-Broadway showing in *Best Foot Forward* carried little weight with the ageing and inflexible Abbott. In any event, his first choice was Eydie Gorme, though it turned out that she was unavailable. But Liza had a strong supporter in the show's lyricist, Fred Ebb, who was not slow to recognize an emerging talent when he saw it. They had first met after *Best Foot Forward* and Ebb had worked with Liza in preparing for her Palladium appearance with Judy.

Ebb recalled years later their first meeting: 'I remember this shy, awkward girl coming into the room. She looked awful, like Raggedy Ann. Everything was just a little torn and a little soiled. She just sat there and stared at me, and I stared back.' Now that he and his partner, John Kander, had produced the score for the new show, Ebb's opinion was not to be dismissed out of hand, though in the end just how influential he was in effecting Abbott's change of mind is not certain. Maybe in looking around there just didn't appear to be much choice and Liza herself would hint later that her own determination to secure the role had a strong bearing on the course of events, claiming that she just kept on plugging away because she wanted the part so much. One thing is certain: the friendship with Fred Ebb would blossom over the years, the talented songwriter and his partner John Kander becoming sufficiently close professionally to become a major influence on Liza's career.

Flora, The Red Menace was not destined to set Broadway alight, but this new musical, brought to the stage in an effort to break away from the tedious run of conventional musical offerings, nevertheless provided an enormous boost to the career of Liza Minnelli, while at the same time helping her establish her own professional persona. Critics were willing to concede for the first time, even if grudgingly, that here was an individual talent after all, despite her famous lineage. She might have some of the looks of her famous mother; there was no concealing the similarity with Judy's stunning voice and her belting delivery; and her breathless energy and highly-charged stage presence bore a striking resemblance to Judy: but for all that, Liza Minnelli was different, far from content to be seen and accepted as a second generation carbon copy of Mama, even a good one.

The show opened at the famous Alvin Theatre in New York on Tuesday, 11 May 1965 after a number of out-of-town try-outs and re-writes extending over more than a month. It was not a commercial success, hampered as it was by the difficult process of transformation from the book to the musical stage. And the public never really took to the story of an impressionable young art student who, soon after graduating, meets a young man, played by Bob Dishy, under whose influence she becomes an enthusiastic advocate of communism. But despite having two big dance routines cut from the show, Liza personally did well from *Flora, The Red Menace*. She was billed as Broadway's newest star.

Reviews were generally favourable and perhaps none would please her more than this from the *World Telegram and Sun*: 'Liza is individual, unduplicated, electrifying — she will be a star on her own terms.' Others she would note with joy and gratitude included: 'Liza triumphs in her brilliant Broadway debut, singing and acting like a polished veteran' and 'Liza, who no longer needs to be identified as Judy Garland's daughter and I apologise for just having done so, has many a fetching way about her.'

The important *Time* magazine couldn't have done more had Liza written the review herself: 'At nineteen, Liza Minnelli is a star-to-be, a performer of arresting presence who does not merely occupy the stage, but fills it.' But *Newsweek* made sure her feet were kept firmly on the ground with this demoralising appraisal: ' . . . her voice is thin, her movements stiff, her presence wobbly and uncertain.' Other happy reviews, however, included 'Liza brings her youth and eagerness to bear on the title role. She has a quality of her own . . . '; 'Liza is impressive in Flora. She should be around a long time'; 'Liza has a good belting voice, a lot of youthful zest and a great deal of charm'; and 'Liza triumphs! A bundle of dynamite rocked the house as Liza made a blessing, crushing Broadway bow.'

The show survived eleven weeks and eighty-seven performances before closing on Saturday, 24 July 1965. By then even Liza's Tony Award as the Best Musical Actress of the Year, announced in June, had failed to give the box office receipts enough of a boost to keep the show going. But for all its shortcomings and relative failure as a Broadway musical show, *Flora, The Red Menace* was to remain something special in the career of Liza Minnelli, for at nineteen she became the youngest performer ever to win a Tony.

The original cast recording of *Flora* was released in America in July 1965 with Liza featured on all tracks. Solos were 'All I Need' (is one good break), 'The Flame', 'Palomino Pal', 'A Quiet Thing', 'Dear Love', 'Express Yourself', 'Knock Knock' and 'Sing Happy'. She shared 'Not Every Day of the Week' and 'Sign Here' with her co-star Bob Dishy.

In the 1960s Liza's status as a club, cabaret and arena performer grew considerably, with Fred Ebb stamping his continuing influence on her career after *Flora* closed by working out a nightclub act with her which she would use with outstanding success. In 1966 in a sensational cabaret debut she broke all existing records at the Shoreham Hotel in Washington DC. Other engagements that year included the Talk of the Town in London, the Coconut Grove in Los Angeles and the Plaza Hotel in New York where, in the Persian Room, she was a sell-out success. That same year she could command $30,000 a week at the Sahara Hotel in Las Vegas.

At the same time her prestige in the recording field continued to rise. In October 1965 Capitol released in America, *Judy Garland and 'Liza Minnelli' Live at the London Palladium*, reissued as a single LP some eight years later, with the British release coming in September 1973. *There is a Time* came out in December 1966 and won the Best Album of the Year award from *Hi-Fi Stereo Review Magazine*. Of the ten tracks the best known were probably 'I Who Have Nothing', 'M'Lord', 'One of Those Songs' and 'Stairway to Paradise'. The release was completed with 'Watch What Happens', 'Days of the Waltz', 'Ay Mariete', 'Love at Last', 'See the Old Man' and 'Parisians'. There were two further LP offerings of Liza in the 1960s. A cast album of television's *The Dangerous Christmas of Little Red Riding Hood* was released by ABC in January 1966. The show had actually taken place in November 1965 and should have scored well since celebrated writers Jule Styne and Bob Merrill provided the songs and Liza co-starred with Vic Damone, Cyril Richard and The Animals. But it missed out and Liza was seen as lacking experience in off-hand comedy. In May 1968 there was, simply, *Liza Minnelli* issued by A & M. Tracks here were 'Debutante's Ball', 'Happyland', the well-known 'Look of Love', 'Butterfly McHeart', 'Waltzing for My Friend', 'Married', 'You'd Better Sit Down', 'Kids', 'So Long Dad', 'Nor No One', 'My Mammy' and 'Happy Times'. Towards the end of the 1960s four of Liza's albums were selling well.

In the 1960s Liza was also very much a globe-trotting artist and in 1967 her programme included an engagement at the Olympia in Paris and a personal invitation from Princess Grace to appear at an important charity ball in Monaco.

Towards the end of the decade Liza and her mother were astride a metaphoric see-saw. Liza's career was strongly in the ascendancy and, though still to make her mark in pictures, she was financially extremely comfortably off. In contrast Judy's life was in tatters. Her movie career had ended with the release in 1963 of the mediocre *A Child is Waiting* and *I Could Go On Singing*, and her private life was a shambles. Her continuing drug and drink problems were not helped by her separation from Mark Herron, which would lead to an acrimonious divorce, and in spite of the vast money she had earned during the early part of her career, and a number of successful and profitable cabaret and theatre dates in more recent times, she was out of money. Liza reportedly helped her out financially more than once. The signs were threatening and it began to look as if Judy's see-saw would never swing upwards again.

While the instinctive affection which Liza had for Judy would remain strong, she now had a career of her own to develop, and inevitably the two were not seeing as much of each other, and were becoming less involved in one another's lives. Liza was busy touring on the strength of her success in *Flora* and, particularly, because of the impact she was making in personal appearances and on record. But she was still looking for that all-important breakthrough on Broadway and had yet to convince Hollywood that she was worthy of some attention from a major studio. Further inroads on Broadway, too, seemed unattainable when a bitterly disappointed Liza missed out on an upcoming stage version of *Cabaret*, but the inkling of a break in movies showed when she was cast in a cameo role in a new British production called *Charlie Bubbles*.

The film was produced by Michael Medwin, whose long-standing friendship with Judy led to Liza being cast as the secretary and mistress of Albert Finney, one of Britain's 'angry young men' of the 1960s. Mind you, Liza was wise enough to know that all producers are tough and although they can have their attention focused, you've got to be able to deliver the goods to get the job. Finney not only directed the picture but took the leading role as Charlie Bubbles, an ex-working class writer who surrenders his professional integrity for money and in so doing acquires many of the neuroses of the rich and famous.

Finney was a major name in the 1960s and Liza was delighted to secure the role, travelling to England where she was met by the British star at London's Heathrow Airport. The film, when released in the UK in 1968, was well received by the critics, but it failed to register commercially in either Britain or the USA. But Liza was still learning the business and the experience was valuable. Recalled James Robert Parish and James Arno in Liza, *Her Cinderella Nightmare*: 'Liza may have been too eager to score in her first film. "You have a face that registers everything," Finney alerted her. "It's not veiled enough. Do half of what you're doing." It was advice which Liza would remember when doing future screen roles.'

Liza's difficulty in breaking into films was largely because there was little suitable material being produced at the time. She was pigeon-holed as a singer and dancer and there just weren't many film musicals being made. In the meantime, however, Liza and Peter Allen had continued their relationship and on Friday, 3 March 1967 they were married at a private ceremony at the Park Avenue, New York home of Liza's agent, Stevie Phillips. She was almost twenty-one, he was twenty-two. Both Judy and Vincente were present at the ceremony — the first time they had been seen together in sixteen years — along with Peter's parents and his sister, Lynn. But the story goes that Judy was so broke at the time that she couldn't afford to get her daughter a wedding present. She bought Liza an Irish linen table cloth and charged it to her account at a store in Beverly Hills, knowing that there would be little chance of the account ever being settled. Lorna and Joey arrived in New York for the ceremony by air from California, courtesy of Liza's own bank account. After the wedding the small group retired to the Central Park West apartment of Liza's married business manager, Martin

Bregman, for a lavish reception.

Liza's career continued at an optimistic level. She had perhaps done enough in *Charlie Bubbles* to catch the eye for, in March 1968, she was invited by producer/director Alan J. Pakula to screen test for the lead in a new project he had in mind for Paramount. She was excited at the opportunity to play 'Pookie' Adams in *The Sterile Cuckoo*, but nothing happened for a long time while Liza continued with her cabaret and concert performances, accepting only short-term engagements just in case Pakula's project came through.

In June she travelled to Australia for a three-week engagement in Sydney and in July, while in Las Vegas, looked set to secure the female lead in a lavish Broadway production of *Promises, Promises*, the first stage musical from the Burt Bacharach/Hal David team, with the famous David Merrick producing. It looked an outstanding opportunity, but against all expectations Liza turned it down, still hoping that Pakula's project would materialize. It was a courageous thing to do, misguided some would say, but Liza was willing to back what was only the possibility of a starring role in a Hollywood movie against the near certainty of a smash hit on Broadway. It showed just how determined she was to make it in pictures. Judy strongly denounced Liza's obsession with the movie project as insanity, being unable to comprehend that her daughter should turn down a near certain hit on Broadway for what she considered could be no more than a mediocre role in a 'B' movie.

There would be plenty of time for Liza to question her own judgement as the project was delayed. First, important areas of doubt developed about the Pakula project itself. It appears that Paramount were uneasy about Pakula taking on the twin responsibilities of producer and director. His skills as a producer where not under question, but they were uncertain about his taking on additional responsibilities as director. More important for Liza was the studio's strong opposition to her taking the lead, citing her limited experience in movies as the reason.

But as preparations began to take

shape Pakula was uncompromising in his insistence that Liza be cast in the top role and in the end, when production work began in the late summer of 1968, Liza Minnelli's was the name to receive top billing, immediately below the title. Her fee was negotiated at $25,000. Liza starred alongside Wendell Burton, Tim McIntire, Austin Green and Sandra Faison in a story about the first sexual experiences of a talkative, but insecure, college girl. It would be the first picture in which she could be seriously measured as a dramatic actress.

The film, put out as *Pookie* in Britain, was not a critical or commercial hit and while Liza's portrayal of a weird, funny and endearing American girl forcing a college love affair on a reluctant student was praised for its portrayals of insecurity and vulnerability, her non-stop talking and emotionalism in what ultimately was considered to be a somewhat tiresome comedy drama, was considered excessive. For all that, Liza's own performance was good enough to put her in line for an Academy Award as she displayed her capacity to shift mood with conviction — all-embracing exuberance in a romp on the beach; startling frankness as she embarrasses Jerry (played by Burton); and melancholia as when, in bed with Jerry, she becomes worried that their relationship may not last.

One of the scenes responsible for the Academy Award nomination, according to James Robert Parish and James Arno, was a warm-hearted seduction sequence between the eager Pookie and the shy Jerry. 'The scene was shot in a seedy motel room at Sylvan Beach, a declining resort community on Lake Oneida in up-state New York. It was October and the chill winds from the lake and the shoddiness of the surroundings enabled Liza and Burton to set the screen aglow with their largely improvised enactment of an experience, the loss of innocence, that comes to almost everyone.'

In the end Liza missed out on an Oscar, but John Douglas Eames in *The Paramount Story* some years later put forward a telling commentary on the film with this assessment: 'Alas, the Alvin Sargent screenplay from John Nicholson's story couldn't make use of Liza's dazzling song-and-dance talents, and the public waited for *Cabaret*.'

But while the public waited for *Cabaret*, Liza made haste. *The Sterile Cuckoo* wouldn't be released until the end of 1969, to be premiered in Britain in February 1970, but by mid-summer 1969 she was already at work on her next starring role in producer-director Otto Preminger's *Tell Me That You Love Me, Junie Moon*, again for Paramount. This time her fee was $50,000 and, despite strong studio efforts to tie her in to a future commitment, Liza insisted on negotiating a one-picture-only deal. However, all told, it seemed that Liza would be having little luck with her choice of picture material, for in addition to its grotesque title, the storyline by Marjorie Kellogg from her own book was hardly calculated to develop a crisis of anticipation among filmgoers.

'A disfigured girl, played by Liza, sets up house with a homosexual paraplegic and an introverted epileptic (together uncharitably described by one critic as a "motley crew of misfits") in an attempt to ameliorate each other's hang-ups,' was a fitting description of the somewhat 'unpalatable plot' comment of another critic. The whole concept never looked like striking a popular chord with the fans and there was little hope from the outset that they would be queuing ten deep at the box office. Preminger was nonetheless able to coax a series of moving portrayals in a film which delivered more than the screenplay and its off-putting title seemed to promise. The earlier part of the film presents some high drama. The disfigured Junie Moon is being discharged from hospital, but once her bandaging is removed, the trauma she experiences at seeing the extent of her injuries as she gazes almost in disbelief into the mirror brings back the memories of her horrific experience, presented in a flashback. We see her going out on a casual date with Jesse. They go dancing, and Junie Moon becomes flirtatious and provocative. She continues to excite Jesse as they drive away from the dance, arousing him with kisses and hugs while he is driving. He stops the car, which is a preliminary to the film's so-called notorious sex scene in the cemetery, but once on the road again Jesse becomes incensed when Junie begins taunting and ridiculing him for his creepy behaviour. This sends Jesse wild. He brings the car to a screeching halt, drags Junie out of the car and into the teeming rain, knocks her to the ground, and repeatedly strikes her while she screams for him to stop. As she remains prostrate on the mud-soaked ground, paralyzed with fear, dazed and hurt, he yanks the battery out of the car and, by now revealed as dangerously psychotic, cracks the battery open and pours acid on her hand, arm and face. Pretty heavy stuff for 1970.

But for all its comparative insignificance as a movie, *Tell Me That You Love Me, Junie Moon* was to stand apart forever from everything she had done or was to do in the future. For it was the movie Liza was making when she received the fateful news that her mother had died.

5

Farewell Mama

IT was hard for Liza to take in the news. Her first thoughts were of concern for her father. Nothing could happen to Mama. She was only 47, one of life's survivors, indestructible. After completing *The Sterile Cuckoo (Pookie)*, which would not be released for another six months, Liza was already committed to *Tell Me That You Love Me, Junie Moon*, but was enjoying a weekend break in Long Island with husband Peter Allen, his sister and a friend.

Peter took the call. Then walked into the bedroom to Liza and said he had something to tell her. She knew it was bad news and, after the shocked numbness which came with Peter's announcement that Judy was dead, Liza somehow knew instantly, instinctively and with uncanny certainty that her mother would never have deliberately taken her own life. Despite all Judy's suicide attempts and her countless periods of black depression, Liza continued courageously and dogmatically to discount the possibility of suicide when later she was confronted by scandal-probing journalists. The official report of the British coroner would afterwards confirm her instinct: Judy's death had been caused by an accidental overdose of the barbiturate, Seconal.

The tragedy occurred at Judy's small mews house in London's Cadogan Lane, close to fashionable Sloane Square, where her body was found shortly after 10 a.m. on Sunday, 22 June 1969, London time. It was in London, only three months before, that Judy had married for the fifth time. Her marriage to her fourth husband, Mark Herron, had been unsteady almost from the start and they had separated after only six months, a swift divorce following. Her new husband, Mickey Deans, owned a nightclub in London and he and Judy had set up home in the capital. Though invited to both Judy's recent weddings, Liza didn't make either. Busy with her own career, Liza had turned down one of the invitations with a jokey 'Not this time Mama, next time, eh?'

Deans had been acting as Judy's agent and manager, but although she was probably more loved in London than anywhere else in the world — she said she had found peace in London — it was becoming desperately hard to pull together the remnants of her disintegrating career. Liza hadn't spent much time with her mother in recent months. She had last seen her briefly in New York earlier in June when Deans persuaded Judy to fly with him to America to discuss the idea of setting up a chain of Judy Garland cinemas.

Like so many ideas for Judy, it came to nothing and Liza was disturbed to find her mother different from her usual ebullient self. The zest for life had gone, the passion, the energy and that inner strength and courage. She seemed demoralized. Her career had run its course and Liza would discover that she and Deans were virtually penniless at the time of her death.

Deans had found the body. A friend

of Judy's had called from America and Mickey said he would have Judy call him back. He went to the bathroom to tell Judy about the call, but found the door locked. When he managed to gain entry, through a fanlight window, he saw her slumped on the toilet seat. He tried to rouse her, but she was already dead. He called an ambulance and Judy was carried from her home for the last time.

Not surprisingly, when Liza called him from New York Deans appeared devastated and unsure, incapable even of making suitable arrangements for the funeral. Liza took over, conquering her stress and natural anxiety, fully determined that her mother would be buried suitably and with dignity. She made all the arrangements, called her father to tell him the news and keeping in close touch with him in the days that followed. She also called Lorna, then sixteen, and Joey, both of whom were in California, to make sure they were all right. It was a gruelling, demanding, emotional and tearful time, but Liza, then only twenty-three herself, found the physical and psychological strength to cope with everything that needed to be done. Somehow she insisted on continuing with her work on *Junie Moon*, though the studio suggested she take some time off. The only day she had away from the studio was the day of the funeral.

After the autopsy at London's Westminster Hospital and the inquest which followed on 25 June, Judy's body was flown to America. Liza and her godmother and close family friend Kay Thompson met the plane at Kennedy Airport a little after midnight and greeted the grieving Deans.

After some disagreement over the funeral arrangements, Liza had her way and arranged for Judy's final resting place to be New York, though Deans insisted on a traditional burial. Liza would have arranged for Judy to be cremated, which she said was what her mother had wanted, but relented under pressure from Sid Luft, not wishing to upset Lorna and Joey further. Judy's death had caused the American nation to falter and for twenty-four hours her fans were given the opportunity of filing quietly past the open coffin, in which Judy lay under a glass covering, at the Frank E. Campbell funeral home in Manhattan. During the hours of daylight and throughout the night, approaching 22,000 people paid their last respects. It was an impressive homage to a much-loved star. Nothing like it had been seen since the passing of silent celluloid hero Rudolph Valentino more than forty years before.

The death of Judy Garland was accepted throughout the world as the passing of a legend in entertainment. The child star in vaudeville who had crooned make-believe songs at three, and became a major Hollywood star before she was sixteen, had carried the profound loyalty of her fans through to the bitter end of her agonized life. Even the sensation of her death was unable to compete with the psychodrama of her life. For many close to her, Judy's premature death was not totally unexpected. Yet for all her fame as one of Hollywood's greatest 'greats' over so many years, she never won an Oscar as an adult. Her consolation had to be the special miniature Oscar she received for her outstanding performance as a screen juvenile during 1939, when she was seventeen.

It is said that in the late 1930s Judy had been offered close to $100,000 a year average for seven years, yet when she died there were no trust funds in place and nothing there for Liza or, indeed, Lorna or Joey. Her legacy of debt was variously reported at between $1 million and $4 million.

A 40-minute funeral service was held on Friday, 27 June with many of Hollywood's greatest names present including Frank Sinatra, Burt Lancaster, Katherine Hepburn, Jack Benny, Cary Grant and Lauren Bacall. Liza's favourite 'uncle', Sammy Davis Jnr, was there, as was Judy's co-star from those early youth musicals, Mickey Rooney. Ray Bolger, the original scarecrow from *The Wizard of Oz*, was present. So was former child star Freddie Bartholomew, who had co-starred with Judy way back in 1938. Two of her five husbands, Sid Luft and Mickey Deans, were present.

Complying with the wishes of Judy, no-one wore black. In acknowledgement of Judy's greatest dramatic, and perhaps also musical, success on film, her co-star from *A Star is Born*, James Mason, flew over from his home in Switzerland to deliver a moving eulogy. Mourners then sang 'The Battle Hymn of the Republic', reprising Judy's own tribute on television following the assassination of John Kennedy. Judy Garland, one of Hollywood's greatest legends, was laid to final rest in Ferncliffe Cemetery in Hartsdale, just a few minutes distance from Scarsdale, where Liza had attended school.

Liza had loved her mother deeply, though had seen less of her during the final months of her deteriorating life. Powerless to help, as Judy's fourth marriage to Mark Herron collapsed, Liza had witnessed with anguish her mother's pathetic attempts to salvage the dregs of a once-proud and internationally-admired talent. But now was the time for Liza to put the record straight, to show that despite Judy's tortured and, for the most part, emotionally unstable life, with its traumatic and sometimes violent repercussions for those around her, she was still her mother, a mother she not only loved but admired and respected with a great deal of understanding and humility.

Her comments were warm and forgiving, with no mention of her own difficulties as the first-born of Judy Garland, international superstar. She said: 'It was her love of life that carried her through everything. The middle of the road was never for her. It bored her. She wanted the pinnacle of excitement. If she was happy, she wasn't just happy — she was ecstatic. And when she was sad, she was sadder than anybody.' She would mention her mother's impatient streak to live; that she had lived eighty lives in one. 'Yet I thought she would outlive us all. She was a great star and a great talent and for the rest of my life I will be proud to be Judy Garland's daughter.'

Judy would have been pleased and proud of such words and could indeed rest in peace. There is no doubt that Liza was emotionally affected by Judy's death, yet there must also have been a sense of freedom and release which Liza felt for both of them. For in the end it seemed inevitable that only death could drive the demons from Judy's soul. Her life had become a wreck. She had suffered enough, partly because of other people, but also through her own almost pathological drive towards self-destruction. Now the tragedy of her life was over. For Liza there was to develop a growing sense of personal and professional freedom. She would never want to hide the fact that she was Judy Garland's daughter, but perhaps she would now be able to begin to live more as Liza Minnelli.

After the funeral a few close friends went with Liza to her East Side apartment for food and drink prepared by Kay Thompson and there to celebrate the life of Judy Garland. Then for Liza there was a film to be made, and she continued with *Junie Moon*. There were high expectations for the movie. Marjorie Kellogg's screenplay, devised from her own successful book, seemed worthy enough and director/producer Otto Preminger had an impressive history of movie-making which included the immensely successful *Laura* in 1944 and

The Man with the Golden Arm some ten years later. He picked Liza for the female lead because of her performance in *The Sterile Cuckoo*, which was released four months after Judy's death, though in this film there was no singing part for Liza. He was convinced, however, that she was on the verge of a major breakthrough and that his picture would make her into a fully-fledged dramatic Hollywood star. But it was not for nothing that Preminger had acquired the reputation for being one of the most controversial figures in American cinema, and Liza would not be the first actress to find the autocratic, ex-Viennese exile, difficult to work with.

If *Laura* had been a masterpiece, then *Junie Moon* turned out to be a major disappointment. Fifteen years before, Preminger had produced one of the most powerful studies of obsession and paranoia in *Bunny Lake is Missing*, which starred Laurence Olivier, Carol Lynley and Noel Coward. His undoubted expertise nowadays lay in having just a few characters and a single, influential thread of action projected on an intimate scale, but this didn't seem to work so well in *Junie Moon*.

On a personal level Liza encountered one or two setbacks. She was the butt of some ill-informed criticism when the film required her to play a sex scene in a cemetery with the psychotic character of her co-star Ben Piazza. He asks her to take off her clothes. As she does so he gets himself sexually aroused by mouthing obscenities. Not the sort of scene to play while still mourning her mother, ran the complaints. During the filming Liza also suffered an acute and severe attack of kidney stones. She was rushed to hospital and spent the best part of the day having treatment. It also began to emerge that her own marriage to Peter Allen was not as healthy as it might have been. Later on, some commentators would isolate 1969, following the death of Judy, as the period when Liza's own subsequent drink and drug problems began to emerge.

The legacy of her mother's fame would fade only slowly. Audiences would clamour for her to sing her mother's songs, particularly 'Over the Rainbow', and in 1970 she would be horrified to discover that Judy had not yet been properly buried. It seemed that Mickey Deans had agreed to look after the arrangements, but the plot he had selected was costly and there was also a delay over some preparation work. Even assuming that Deans had the best of intentions, the fact was that Judy's body had remained stored in a temporary crypt. When Liza heard about it she immediately paid the outstanding money so that the burial could finally take place, almost seventeen months after Judy's death, on Wednesday, 4 November 1970. It was also in 1970, after the Oscar Ceremony, that Liza announced her separation from Peter Allen.

More than a decade after her death Liza would say that she still thought about her mother a dozen times a day and in some ways she thought her death brought them closer. By then she had also revealed that if she ever had a daughter of her own, she would call her Judy, 'after Mama'.

6

Come to the Cabaret

LOOKING back, it is inconceivable that anyone other than Liza Minnelli should play the part of the mercurial Sally Bowles in *Cabaret*. Yet when Christopher Isherwood's original story of decadent life in pre-second world war Berlin was being reshaped for the Broadway stage, Liza's candidature was dismissed with barely a second thought. The sticking point was not one of suitability or talent. It was decided on nationality. The original idea had Sally as a British girl. There is no-one more 'all-American' than Liza. So Jill Haworth was given the part, after producer Hal Prince backed writer Joe Masteroff's judgment in sticking to authenticity and casting a British girl in the role.

The stage production of *Cabaret* opened on Broadway in 1966 and was the first of a new genre of live

144

musicals having the songs and dances separated from the story. Joel Grey was the Master of Ceremonies. In the later London production Barry Dennen's portrayal was generally accepted as being superior, while Jill Haworth's 'Sally' was less convincing than Judi Dench's characterization in the latter stages of the London production.

Liza was said to be devastated by the decision which eliminated her as a possible for the New York show. She was almost obsessional in wanting the part and had good reason to think she would get it. For not only did she love the show and feel that many of the songs were just right for her kind of voice and personality, but she was already thrilling audiences with her own sizzling cabaret act and had recently proved herself fully on stage in *Flora, The Red Menace*, with that precious Tony award. No-one was in a better position to know all this than *Flora*'s producer, Hal Prince, and songwriters Fred Ebb and John Kander, all of whom were already working on *Cabaret* by the time *Flora* closed. Liza was certain she would get the part and never considered she would fall victim to a technicality. She later insisted that she auditioned fourteen times for this Broadway production, but others close to the show would raise their eyebrows at the claim. It was also reported later that she had auditioned only once, because of Prince's insistence on having a British girl.

But if Liza goes for what she wants with outstanding tenacity and almost limitless physical and mental endurance, she is also a realist. Once she accepted that *Cabaret* on Broadway was a lost cause, she moved on to other things. For almost three years she pursued the role of Pookie Adams in the screen version of John Nichols' novel, *The Sterile Cuckoo*. She was able to thumb her nose at her critics when she was deservedly acclaimed for her portrayal of the immodest yet melancholy student in this Paramount picture; and then won an Academy Award nomination.

But Liza didn't entirely give up on the idea of sometime playing the sexually decadent Sally Bowles. When the screen version was contemplated more than five years later her impact as an international cabaret star and her stronger profile as a screen actress made her an automatic choice. The fact that she was American made no difference this time, for in the cinematic version of the story Sally Bowles was portrayed as an American anyway. But by the time shooting began on *Cabaret* in Munich in February 1971 Liza was a high-profile media name for more than just being an entertainer. She might well have lost the 'daughter of Judy Garland' tag, but she was now becoming equally well-known for her active and predatory love life. The on-off relationship with husband Peter Allen wouldn't end in divorce until 1974, and at the time of *Cabaret* she was reported to have temporarily resumed relations with Peter; but there was continued speculation over her close friendship with lyricist Fred Ebb; and when she went to Germany for the shooting of *Cabaret* she moved into an apartment in the bohemian sector of the town with musician Rex Kramer, a member of her own backup group with whom Liza had been associating for a little while. Maybe she was attracted by someone so different because Kramer was said to be the opposite of Allen. He, unlike Peter, hated city life, but loved the country . . . and girls. The complication romantically was that he too was married. Unlike most of Liza's romances, this one would end far from pleasantly. His wife would later bring the relationship out into the open by claiming in a law suit that Liza had used her position, wealth and influence to entice Kramer away from her. It would be reported that Liza felt cheated and used, wanting to break off the relationship, but for the time being she was reasonably happy to be with Kramer while she concentrated on making the new movie. Allen at the time provided an insight into Liza's 'all or nothing' character. 'She thought she was getting back to her roots, and after that began talking about spending the rest of her life on his (Kramer's) family farm in Arkansas,' he said. But whether Liza was serious is anybody's guess.

However, as Rex grew more possessive he became such an increasing nuisance that he was barred from the set. He had said that he would only leave Liza if she fell in love with someone else, so she and her secretary conspired against him. Like a genie emerging from the lamp, a new love was invented, said to be a cameraman working on the picture.

Cabaret on the big screen had all the makings of being a major success. Bob Fosse was directing and would also choreograph the new film. Already a five-times Tony winner on Broadway and a man of undisputed talent and vision, he moved on to *Cabaret* after creating something of a sensation directing and choreographing the film version of *Sweet Charity* in 1969. In *Cabaret* he would underscore his brilliant artistry in both choreography and film making, which were as dazzling as anything he had done in the past. Liza considered *Cabaret* to be a Fosse masterpiece. Almost twenty years on, in Liza's screen hit *Stepping Out*, when trying to impress a member of her dance class with an outline of her experience in the business, she says proudly ' . . . I even auditioned for Bob Fosse.' Could this have been her subtle way of acknowledging his work on *Cabaret*? Cy Feuer, accomplished producer and director, also with award-winning musicals on Broadway to his credit, would make his film debut as producer on *Cabaret* while Joel Grey, following his triumph in the Broadway stage version, for which he received a Tony, was brought in to recreate, with an incisive and masterly touch, the role of the sardonic, effetely dangerous Master of Ceremonies at the garish and sleazy Kit Kat Klub.

Certainly, Liza was in good company and she dedicated herself to the role, often working fourteen and fifteen hours a day on the set on a portrayal which was physically and psychologically exhausting. The film was shot on location in West Berlin and at Bavaria Ateller Gesellschaft MbH in Munich. The screenplay by Jay Allen, surely the ultimate amalgam of Joe Masteroff's Broadway presentation, John Van Druten's *I am a Camera* and Christopher Isherwood's *Goodbye to Berlin*, gave Liza her most demanding screen role to date. Dance routines were difficult and often energetic, and three of the songs were solo performances, with

'Money, Money, Money' a challenging duet with Joel. The outrageous costumes and freakish make-up with vivid green nail polish, and green eye shadow set against a mousy pale skin and bright red pouty lips, created their own special demands as cabaret singer Sally Bowles sets out to be the symbol of 'divine decadence' in 1930s Berlin — a Berlin where the cafe society acts as a haven from the real world of growing violence, anti-semitism and the emerging Nazi Party.

Cabaret, as might be guessed, is not a musical of gently swaying palms, invigorating mountain air, or even the light, innocent romance of boy meets girl through song and dance. *Cabaret* is a story of grotesque sensibilities, immorality and bizarre images, with a hint of homosexuality, lust, an abortion and even a touch of female mud-wrestling thrown in for good measure. It centres around tangled lives in a city where accepted morality is being flouted. In his book, *History of Movie Musicals*, Thomas G. Aylesworth observed: '*Cabaret* confronted the facts that people use each other, homosexuality exists, Nazism had its seductions, and decadence can be fun. *Cabaret* used music in an exciting new way. Characters did not burst into song to express their emotions; a sleazy nightclub, the Kit Kat Klub, became a place where satirical comment on the lives and problems of the characters was made in striking, entertaining and savage dances and songs.'

But for all its crude gestures and creepy undertones, it was to emerge as a truly great picture. Yet so easily could it have been otherwise. All it needed was for the film-makers to have indulged themselves, to have delved just a little too deeply or a little too gratuitously into the social degeneracy which was essential to the story. But the skill of construction was always there, the restraint of experts at work. Liza's comic sense and basic innocence, despite her fraught lifestyle, contributed hugely to the acceptance factor of what is basically a squalid tale.

The story opens in the vice-ridden Berlin of the 1930s with the Master of Ceremonies, wearing white make-up, rouged lips and jet black plastered hair, enticing patrons to the cabaret at the Kit Kat Klub with his singing and dancing of 'Willkommen'. The temptation on offer is to leave your problems outside, for once inside the Kit Kat Klub all your troubles will disappear. We then see that British language student Brian Roberts (a youthful Michael York) has arrived in Berlin and rents accommodation at the Schneider rooming house. In the next room, complete with wind-up gramophone, lives Sally Bowles, a singer at the Klub with ambitions to become a great actress. She is outrageously out-going with few inhibitions, and Brian has no difficulty in seeing her point when she informs him: 'I'm a strange and extraordinary person.' Brian is quieter, reserved, but is captivated by her exuberance and candour, even in delicate, personal matters. She persuades him to visit the Kit Kat Klub to see her sing 'Mein Herr' and they become friends; soon they are lovers. Brian earns a living in Berlin giving English lessons. His two pupils are Fritz Wendel (Fritz Wepper), a friend of Sally's, and Natalia Landauer (Marisa Berenson), a strikingly beautiful young woman whose family has money. These two are in love, but she refuses to marry him because she is Jewish and believes he is not. This keeps them miserably apart until Brian stumbles into making a dramatic revelation which makes all the difference.

Meantime, Sally has met Baron Maximillan von Heune (Helmut Griem) and is attracted by his handsome looks, cavalier style and his obvious wealth. Sally is impressed by, and drawn to, the Baron as he lavishes gifts on both Sally and Brian, and inevitably she becomes his lover. Brian, Max and Sally stay together at Max's lavish country mansion and drink into the early hours, becoming less inhibited and more intoxicated. When later Sally tells Brian openly that she is Max's lover, Brian shocks Sally by informing her that he also has shared Max's bed. Brian is nonetheless jealous and outraged at Sally's relationship with Max, but when Sally tells him that she is pregnant (she typically hollers out the news through the penetrating stillness of a public library) yet unsure about the father, Brian convinces her that he wants the baby anyway. Sally, however, has an abortion, handing over her prized fur coat in payment.

The story unfolds against the sickly decadence of the Kit Kat Klub and the growing menace of Nazism, but for a time Brian prefers to ignore the brownshirts, banners and outbreaks of anti-Jewish violence, while enjoying life with Sally. But when Sally admits her relationship with Max, Brian storms out and is beaten up by two Nazis when he insults them, ruining their banner. There is also an ominously prophetic scene when Brian, Sally and Max call at a country beer garden. A young German is singing 'Tomorrow Belongs to Me' and the tension mounts as the music becomes stronger and the patrons join in with intense national fervour. In the end Brian decides it is time to leave Berlin. He says goodbye to Sally and after a final embrace she sings the title song 'Cabaret'.

The film was to confirm Liza Minnelli as a major screen star. She created a totally convincing Sally Bowles, a long-legged, provocative cabaret dancer who, despite her moral laxity, manages to emerge as an amazingly sympathetic character. Those enormous eyes, outrageous costumes, almost witch-like hairstyle, aggressive make-up and frenzied energy, fit the bill perfectly for Sally — and Liza too. The songs by John Kander and Fred Ebb captured with intense feeling the creepy atmosphere of those unique times, providing Liza with a magnificent musical score. Of her four featured musical numbers, two would become enormous hits — 'Cabaret' particularly, and 'Money, Money, Money'. Both would significantly expand her name and reputation as a singer while she would go on to stamp her imprimatur on 'Cabaret' almost as strongly as her mother had done with 'Over the Rainbow' all those years before. Though it was perhaps less publicly acclaimed, she also scored heavily in influential musical circles with her handling of 'Maybe This Time'. The sequence of its introduction into the picture is cleverly conceived. It is introduced immediately after she and the very British and correct Michael York have become lovers. Liza starts softly, the tender scenes between them being interspersed with the musical content, but as the song slowly gains in excitement and tension the vision dissolves to a full scale stage performance at the Klub with the Minnelli voice at its most vibrant. She controls her natural exuberance and produces just the right degree of excitement and passion to make her interpretation of this haunting song one of the musical highlights of the picture.

Some of the songs featured in the Broadway version were cut from the movie, but three featured numbers were specially written for Liza by Ebb and Kander, the aforementioned 'Money, Money, Money' and 'Cabaret', along with their earlier composition 'Maybe This Time'; and the film was destined to be judged by many of the high priests of the movie world as perhaps the best musical of the 1970s, despite its narrow, unconventional and extremely chilling focus. In fact its stinging and claustrophobic satire was the very antithesis of the accepted Hollywood musical, and on this basis alone its lavish popular success and critical acclaim was all the more remarkable.

A film exactly right for the time of its release, it received international praise, and Liza's bravura performance is still considered by many critics to be the very best of her career. *Cabaret* gave full expression to her multi-faceted talent — singing, dancing and acting; plus her always exciting and telling 'presence' in front of the camera. There is no doubt that she dominated the picture to become the veritable incarnation of the popular visualization of Sally Bowles. Though some purists may have found the clever blend of natural innocence and calculated guile invoked by her portrayal a little too contemporary and too American to be convincing as the 'divinely decadent' Sally, she was seen by most critics as closer to the real thing than her predecessors on stage, and became for many people the definitive Sally Bowles.

There is no doubt, also, that Liza was supported by a capable and well-chosen cast. British-born Michael York, a product of Britain's National Theatre, had co-starred on screen with Elizabeth Taylor and Richard Burton and in 1966 had achieved enormous success in the UK when he made his television debut as young Jolyon in the BBC's famous adaptation of Galsworthy's *The Forsyte Saga*.

Joel Grey had been in show business for twenty-five years, having started out as an actor at the age of ten. He followed his Tony award for the stage version of *Cabaret* with a Tony nomination for his performance in *George M*, these two musicals setting him up as one of the most sought-after song-and-dance men, a reputation underlined by his Oscar for *Cabaret*. His bizarre make-up for the film was said to have been created to look like cafe performers in the 1930s, when male entertainers used lipstick, rouge and patent-leather hair without discretion. Helmut Griem, chosen to play the wealthy Baron, was one of Germany's finest actors and in 1968 won the Best Actor Award from the Berlin Academy for his performance in *Rosencrantz and Guilderstern*. He won worldwide acclaim for his portrayal of an ardent Nazi in director Luchino Visconti's picture, *The Damned*. Marisa

Berenson, in the role of the wealthy Natalia Landauer affected by changing values in the Berlin of the 1930s, was a world famous model. *Cabaret* was her first starring role. As early as seventeen she had been acclaimed as one of *Vogue*'s top performers and went on to grace the covers of most fashion magazines in the United States and Europe. She would later gain recognition as a member of New York's trendy set, along with Liza, in the peak days of Andy Warhol. Fritz Wepper, as Fritz Wendel, was considered to be one of Europe's most experienced and dedicated actors and was well known on German television as a detective in the country's longest running series, *The Commissar*.

Liza's desperate need to do the part was shown by the way she spent days and weeks researching every aspect of the character, which had been substantially strengthened from the stage role. She immersed herself totally, capturing with an uncanny insight and instinct the bizarre image and eccentric character of the American girl who went to Germany to become a small-time cabaret singer and who relished the freedom and human laxities of pre-second World War Germany. Little could Liza have realized at the time that, having finally put to rest the burden of being Judy Garland's daughter, *Cabaret* would bestow upon her another almost inescapable identity. The film was to become a classic and one of the most successful of all time, and Liza's stunning performance, whether or not she welcomed the claustrophobic connection, would make her as inseparable from *Cabaret* as she had once been from her mother. It was the picture known far and wide for making Liza Minnelli into a Hollywood star.

After completing *Cabaret* Liza returned to a full programme of live concert and cabaret appearances. She completed successful dates in Hollywood, Las Vegas and Lake Tahoe. There followed an engagement in Paris at the Olympia Theatre which brought outstanding press reviews on her talent and personality. She also hit the international gossip column headlines with an assortment of reported romances. There was Baron Alexis de Rede, whom she had known for some time but who, following her triumph at the Olympia, threw a special party in her honour at his seventeenth-century town house in Paris. It was a grand society affair with a galaxy of elitist VIPs present including Richard Burton and Elizabeth Taylor. She was also attracted to Desi Arnaz, Jnr, the son of actor Desi Arnaz and his phenomenally successful wife, Lucille Ball.

They had first met some time earlier, but he came back into her life in a serious way after her engagement at the Greek Theatre in Los Angeles, following her to her concerts in Las Vegas and Lake Tahoe. Seven years younger than Liza, Desi at nineteen years old was already noted for an affair with Hollywood actress Patty Duke. Patty, aged twenty-five, was now claiming that her infant son Sean was fathered by Desi, though she was still married to someone else. Desi proposed to Liza almost immediately, but as she was still married to Peter Allen, the exchange of rings was purely an outward expression of how they felt about one another. Desi's parents, however, were delighted at the new liaison and Lucy took to Liza as if she were her own daughter. But they would never be married.

Both Desi and his father escorted Liza to the gala world premiere of *Cabaret* which was held at the Ziegfeld Theatre in New York. It was a glittering occasion and more exciting than had been expected, for after the first press preview of the film two nights earlier, the word was already out that this was an exceptional movie. Liza was immediately identified as an Academy Award nominee.

The press acclaimed her as the latest superstar. Roger Ebert's report for the *Chicago Sun-Times* was typical: 'Sally is brought magnificently to the screen by Liza Minnelli, who plays her as a girl who's bought what the cabaret is selling. To her, the point is to laugh and sing and live forever for the moment . . . ' It is no exaggeration to say that both musically and dramatically Liza had delivered an exceptional performance and that the picture was acknowledged as one of the best musicals in Hollywood history. Considering that this was only the fourth movie she had made, Liza had every reason to be ecstatic.

The film which had cost a little over $4 million to make would gross more than $18 million in North America alone and would make a fortune for Liza as well as bringing her international stardom. She appeared on the covers of both *Time* and *Newsweek* in the same week, but whether Liza would win an Oscar for her performance was by no means certain. It was a good year for picture-making and she had a lot of tough competition, probably the toughest from an outstanding performance by Diana Ross in *Lady Sings the Blues*, the biopic of blues and jazz singer Billie Holiday.

The evening of the awards was a tense, nervous time for Liza, who attended the presentation ceremony accompanied by her father, who had recently been ill. *Cabaret* was beaten to the Best Picture award by Marlon Brando's *The Godfather*, a powerful drama, and since drama is always preferred over musicals at the Oscar presentations, the result was not unexpected. Brando's Best Actor award was also no surprise. But Liza's confidence was growing for, by the time of the announcement of the Best Actress award, *Cabaret* had already collected five Oscars against *The Godfather*'s two. Liza pipped Diana Ross to the Best Actress award and in accepting her Oscar made the point that this award was *hers* for a performance which *she* had produced. In other words, celebrity lineage and the fact that her mother had been the famous Judy Garland had nothing to do with it.

Further competition for Liza had come from Liv Ullman in *The Emigrants* and Maggie Smith in *Travels with My Aunt*. While *The Godfather* might well have won the Best Picture award, Cabaret collected the lion's share of the spoils. No fewer than eight Oscars would go to *Cabaret* and, in addition to Liza's award, there were major Oscars for Joel Grey (Best Supporting Actor), Bob Fosse (Director), Geoffrey Unsworth (Cinematography), Herbert Strabel (Art Director) and Ralph Burns (Music — Adaptation).

Cabaret had been such an outstanding success that Liza was content to wait for another good film project to come along, deciding meantime to concentrate on public performances. But it must surely have been one of the weirdest quirks of motion picture history that, having been an Academy Award winner in one of the most successful musical films of all time, she had to wait three whole years before anything was offered which motivated her enough to return to filming. Even then perhaps it was more a move of desperation than a tempting project which would bring her back to the big screen, a return which would be singularly disappointing. Oh for the exploitative skills of the big studio days when Garland was riding high! Then, confronted with a movie even half as successful as *Cabaret* and a star as big box-office as Liza Minnelli, a follow-up picture would have been on the stocks almost before the earlier one had been released. How times, even in Hollywood, had changed.

It was two years after *Cabaret* went out on general release that Liza was involved with the novelty sequel to *The Wizard of Oz* when she provided a 'voice over' for *Journey Back to Oz*. In this animated feature Dorothy returns to the land of Oz to discover that the sister of the wicked witch is continuing the evil influence. And Liza was also chosen as one of the narrators for MGM's *That's Entertainment*, a lavish tribute to movie musicals made by the famous studios between the years from 1929 to 1958. Written, produced and directed by Jack Haley Jnr with Daniel Melnick as executive producer, this was a dedication by the cinema to its own success and blended newly-filmed accounts of the personal memories of eleven of the stars who were at MGM during the making of these films with a panoramic retrospective of unforgettable musical sequences from them. But *Journey Back to Oz* and *That's Entertainment*, even together and notwithstanding the latter's popular success, was hardly a worthy follow-up to Liza's international block-buster of only two years before.

In a sense she was part of the latter almost by default, and perhaps mostly as a substitute for her late mother, for she hardly fitted in with the generation of former superstars from whom her co-narrators had been chosen. These were Fred Astaire, Bing Crosby, Gene Kelly, Peter Lawford, Donald O'Connor, Debbie Reynolds, Mickey Rooney, Frank Sinatra, James Stewart and Elizabeth Taylor. Clips and longer sequences from almost sixty films were put together into a rousing musical marathon which included classics from the golden age of the big-scale musicals like *An American in Paris*, *The Band Wagon*, *Babes in Arms*, *Meet Me in St Louis*, *Ziegfeld Follies* and, of course, *The Wizard of Oz*. Not for the first time one was left to ponder the idea that, though born into a later generation, Liza Minnelli had an uncanny affinity for the genre of yesteryear.

But if big screen progress was hard to come by for Liza in the mid to late 1970s, there was little slackening of pace in her already well-reported romantic involvements. Her marriage to Peter Allen had been effectively dead for some time and her infatuation with Rex Kramer was at an end even before shooting had finished on *Cabaret*. For a time her relationship with Desi Arnaz Jnr (they had organized a big celebration to announce their 'engagement' at about the time of the Los Angeles premiere of *Cabaret*), looked strong and might have led to marriage, but it didn't happen. After they parted her name was frequently linked with various minor names in the world of entertainment. Then she made a trip to London in the spring of 1973 to give three performances of her one-woman show at the London Palladium. Now a star in her own right, she enjoyed standing ovations, which enabled the British press to make the most of their opportunities when suddenly they saw what they considered to be a scandal in the very best of show business traditions emerging right on their own doorstep.

For Liza's journey to Britain led her straight into an unexpected torrid and deeply emotional affair with British top celebrity Peter Sellers. It had been a great life for her recently. Now twenty-six, in September 1972 her television special, *Liza With a Z*, was shown by NBC in the US and notched her an Emmy Award. It would become vintage Minnelli because of the title song, a classical, comical tongue-twister in the Danny Kaye style and based on the pronunciation of her first name — 'Ligh-za', not 'Lee-sa'. Four months later she received the Golden Globe Award as Best Actress (comedy or musical) for *Cabaret* and on 27 March 1973 collected her Oscar for the movie. She had plenty to celebrate; and celebrate she did with Sellers.

The affair was instant, undisguised, frenetic and free-spirited, despite the fact that Liza was still legally married to Peter Allen and would not be divorced for more than a year. Sellers also was still legally married; but once news of the affair got out they were hounded by the British tabloids, who had the sniff of scandal in their nostrils, for the romance had the unfailing bonus in media terms of Sellers being twenty years older than Liza. The press had been alerted when Sellers, currently making a film in London, had been seen at one of Liza's shows, obviously enthusiastic and admiring her performance. Almost immediately they began to be seen openly in London, walking in the park, affectionate at smart restaurants and in hotel lobbies. She visited him during filming at Shepperton studios. Liza moved out of her hotel and into Peter's apartment and the infatuation seemed intense as Liza announced that she was in love with him and he with her.

Then something happened. Liza moved back into the Savoy and an obviously less-happy Sellers was spotted later leaving her suite. Sustained press interest ruined her intention of taking a house in London and living there quietly for a time, and in the end she admitted it was all over, without giving any reason, except to say ' . . . I have no regrets; how can you regret anything that was so happy.' The explosive affair had lasted about five weeks. From what Liza had to say about it later, the relationship seems to have been serious and genuine, while Sellers had at one time talked to the press about marriage once they became clear of their present legal partners.

Later, back in the United States, there was a short and none too successful reconciliation with Dezi Arnaz Jnr, and after a brief trip abroad to entertain American troops in the Far East, she resumed her successful concert career, receiving a reputed $300,000 for just three weeks at Broadway's Winter Garden in New York. All available seats were taken within thirty-six hours of tickets becoming available and the show was an enormous success. Liza was always concerned to give the punters value for money and this occasion was no exception. She swept from one song to the next, displaying a remarkable touch for standards from her late mother's era as well as more contemporary compositions. There were dance numbers, happy chatter, an extraordinary relationship with her audience and an overall presentation which never once faltered. The engagement grossed over $413,000, constituting something of a record, and her special midnight charity performance on 25 January, benefited the Actors' Fund by more than $21,000. But despite such triumphs, Liza was desperate to follow up with another big picture success and aching to work with her father. The fan magazines had already talked of one or two possibilities. She was said to be on the verge of signing for a screen update of the classic *Camille*, though not with her father but with the well known Italian director, Franco Zeffirelli. Then reports filtered through that Vincente might after all become involved with the project. But there was no immediate development on this or any other possibility. The question was beginning to be asked: did Hollywood want Liza Minnelli after all? Despite her credentials as a dramatic actress following *Cabaret*, was she too much of a song-and-dance lady at a time when song-and-dance pictures weren't being made any more?

Meantime, she continued to score heavily with stage and theatre audiences, adding 'Cabaret' and other songs from her cinema success to her repertoire. She was now considered one of the most exciting 'live' entertainers in the world, capable of commanding huge fees for personal appearances and theatre and nightclub dates at all the major venues in North America and throughout Europe. She had also, it seemed, completely extinguished any possible embers which might have remained from her affair with Peter Sellers, for before the aforementioned

173

Winter Garden engagement she went around with Ben Vereen, the black star from the successful Broadway show, *Pippin*, though Liza insisted that they were just friends. When he moved out of focus, Edward Albert Jnr took over and this seemed to be more serious, since there was once again talk of marriage, though Peter and Liza were still officially man and wife.

But not for much longer. Although they had been married for almost seven years, the divisions had developed comparatively early on, driven on at that time by the way Liza's career was moving ahead strongly while Peter's seemed to be stagnant. The wonder is that it lasted so long, but when Liza had grabbed at the opportunity to become involved as a narrator for MGM's *That's Entertainment*, it brought her into contact with the film's producer, Jack Haley Jnr. The two had known one another as children, for Jack's father, Jack Haley, had played the Tin Man in Judy Garland's spectacular success *The Wizard of Oz* more than thirty years before. They had met more recently when he directed the 1973 Academy Awards show, for which he had suggested she do a 'spectacular'. They quickly became engaged and by early 1974, according to the gossips, she had moved into his Los Angeles home.

The romance blossomed and this time seemed more deep-rooted, particularly when later that year Liza broke the news that she and Haley would be married. This time Peter seemed less upset and more resigned to the inevitable. His classic quote from that time said it all: 'When you're been separated longer than you were married, it's time to get a divorce.' But this time there was none of the flamboyance or naked contempt for public opinion which had characterised her brief relationship with Peter Sellers. Nor was there any calculated duplicity. Shortly after the start of divorce proceedings she embarked on a major European concert tour. Liza and Peter Allen were divorced on 24 July 1974 and a few weeks later, on 15 September, she and Jack Haley Jnr, his earlier reported affairs with Carole Lynley and Nancy Sinatra set aside, were married at a quiet ceremony at a small Presbyterian Church close to Santa Barbara in California, with nine family guests and friends present including Sammy Davis Jnr, who was best man. Haley Jnr was 41, Liza was 28.

7

The Lady Known as Liza

THE baby born to be a star was a young woman nudging thirty by the mid-1970s, small to medium height with a good figure, vivacious personality and a hectic lifestyle. She was self-deprecating about her looks, accepting she was no traditional beauty from the classic days of celluloid Hollywood. But her beautiful brown eyes were strikingly large and combined with a personality and presence strong enough to pick her out at the most crowded and glamorous of occasions.

Without being a martyr to the cause she conveyed an easy-going, almost instinctive acceptance of sexual equality which left her the freedom to start friendships as naturally with men as with women. There had been a variety of reported romances during her teens and twenties and by thirty she had been married and divorced. Professionally the comparisons with Judy were still inevitable, though less so now that her enormous and exciting individual talent was not in doubt. *Cabaret* in 1972 brought her not only the distinction of an Oscar, but cast aside any lingering uncertainty that here was a performer of class, stature and maturity.

While she was destined to drift into a lifestyle she found difficult to control, fearfully raising the spectre of her mother's tragedy, the high standards she had set herself as an entertainer were never under threat. She would say some years later, when looking back to the disaster of *Rent-A-Cop*: 'You have no idea at the time and can't blame anyone. You just say, "Next time I will do better". I'm a perfectionist, which is a pain but something I accept and just hope that I don't become too obsessive. You have to follow your heart.'

At thirty she was well on the way to becoming what is known in the business as a trouper, a convenient tag-line which reaches back with reverence to the time-honoured traditions of vaudeville and silent movies. Though part of a new age when electronic gadgetry and crazy looks would count for more than a good voice and evident talent, Liza none the less would cling instinctively to the values of her mother's generation. 'For my whole life,' she would say, 'I've been singing songs written before I was born.' And even in the late 1980s when she successfully ventured into what was for her the no-man's-land of rock music, she would nail her contemporary flag to time-honoured values: 'People seem to think this is a huge departure for me,'she would explain. 'It's not. It's still about singing good songs.'

Over the years it became clear that Liza was the product of the way she was brought up. Judy certainly didn't go by the book, thumbing the pages of a 'what to do' manual to see her through the minefield of her daughter's adolescence. Liza, too, learned about life as she went along and in many instances was sensible enough to benefit from her parents' mistakes. Not that she blamed them for anything. In fact, given the circumstances of her childhood, it points to her generosity of spirit that over the years she has vigorously defended her parents against any suggestion that they have been the cause of some of her own problems. She will sweep aside with the same absence of compromise anyone inclined to dwell mawkishly on her mother's tragic life. Despite the onset of her own drink and drug problems, she has thankfully never suffered the terrible emotional blackouts she had witnessed as a child in her mother.

Mind you, looking at and listening to Liza as she scaled the precipitous face of showbiz, it was hard to keep the fading snapshots of Judy from one's mind. There were the same mannerisms, the nervous gestures, the underlying high-tension volatility struggling to be kept under control and, above all perhaps, the energy and enthusiasm of Judy at her best. Liza can sing almost any song and emerge with her reputation intact. She has never been known as a sex symbol, yet when she wishes it, no other actress's body language conveys a greater degree of subtle sensuality. Liza's dark brown saucer eyes are bigger than

On the blackboard:

FITTINGS

J. Leigh – 2:30
L. Minnelli – 4:30
G. Garson – 1:30
J. Mason – 11:00

All dressed up and somewhere to go. Not yet three years old, but the infant trouper is ready to make her mark in *In The Good Old Summertime*, which starred her mother and Van Johnson.

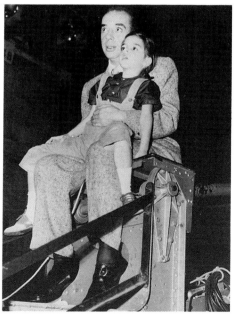

There was no greater childhood thrill than to be taken onto the film set by her director father Vincente Minnelli. Early memories to be treasured forever.

As Sally Bowles in *Cabaret* in 1972,
still vividly remembered for her outstanding all-round
performance which won her an Oscar.

Growing up fast. There was never any doubt that Liza would follow her talented parents and become a professional entertainer.

Playing British actor Albert Finney's secretary *Charlie Bubbles*, her first feature film released in 1968.

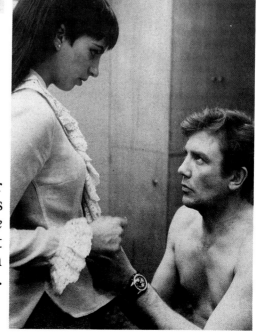

Judy was a continuing influence on her career and her life. Starstruck as a toddler on the set with her mother and Mickey Rooney.

Happy with the Australian entertainer Peter Allen. He became her first husband in 1967, just one week before she was twenty-one.

Judy's, her neck longer and more elegant, she grew to be prettier than her mother, and has longer and shapelier legs. In a rare moment of self assessment she would tell a journalist: 'Many people say my tits are my best feature, but I think my legs are better.'

Certainly she is more poised, much more often in control than Judy. Her high level of energy comes from her underlying nervous tension. She developed a dual personality which makes her tough yet vulnerable, calm yet excitable. Friends will tell you that despite her balanced ambience of worldly experience, excitability, personal magnetism, lavish personality and her 'always in charge' professional persona, they can't help but feel protective towards her. Somehow, as Joel Grey once said, she is capable of making you care about her. 'But then you realize she is perfectly capable of looking after herself.' Loyalty is also a strong point with her. Many of her friends and associates have been close to her all her life. Fred Ebb once said that if Liza respected you she would follow you over a cliff. She enjoys getting on with people and once confessed that she hates scenes and will do almost anything to avoid them.

She inherited the strong singing voice of Judy, if not the range in the upper register, and even if the voice sometimes lacks the rounded melodious qualities of Judy on top form, there is the same distinctive vibrato, blistering delivery and occasional coltish giggle. On stage she is not always a subtle performer. She gyrates a lot, is unconventional, gets emotional and excitable, and often leads her audiences to the foothills of poor taste, sentimentality, even embarrassment — but never a step further. Privately she has become known as an habitual nail-biter, tearing through life like an express train, and while she has successfully kicked the twin Frankensteins of booze and pills, her voracious smoking has never been defeated.

In the late 1970s and early 1980s she was more famous as a party-goer than as a film actress. She relished living in New York and told *Photoplay*, pointing up the differences between herself and Streisand: 'I enjoy contact with fans and street life and the parties and discos.'

She also relished moving in on the fringe of New York's contemporary society. It was following the making of *Cabaret* that Liza hitched herself to the aesthete bandwagon, mixing with some of the extreme elements of the fashion-fetish 'in' crowd, forgetting work and career for a while. Cabaret star and former fashion model, Marisa Berenson, who had been brought up in the rarified atmosphere of the pure arts, was Liza's carpet-ride to this new and abstract world. Marisa's grandfather, who died in 1959, was the American art historian Bernard Berenson. His works had set new standards of criticism and he was notable for his authorship of the definitive *Italian Painters of the Renaissance*.

Caught up in the subculture of the city's art, fashion and music colony, Liza was on a dangerous merry-go-round from which she found it hard to escape. Her general condition wasn't helped by the Valium prescribed for her scoliosis condition. She was part of New York's 'cool' crowd, the power people of Studio 54 during the days of

Halston, Calvin Klein, Mick and Bianca Jagger, rubbing shoulders with all sorts of magical names including the Rothschilds, Salvador Dali and Yves Saint-Laurent. She was also led into the unreal world of pop artist Andy Warhol, noted for his imagery taken from advertisements of, most famously, Coca-Cola bottles and Campbells soup cans.

Originally a commercial artist, Warhol had achieved notoriety in the 1960s for, soup cans and bottles apart, his portraits of film stars, notably Marilyn Monroe, and his erotic and controversial films *Sleep* (1963) and *Chelsea Girls* (1966). During the late 1970s Liza was living in the fast lane, one of Studio 54's 'gang of four' along with Bianca, Halston and Warhol; she was photographed sedately kissing the narcissistic artist at his Broadway studio known as 'The Factory'. Liza liked the eccentric Warhol, but didn't forgive him for his revealing diaries published posthumously, which referred to her alleged affairs with Martin Scorsese and others, and hinted at other minor scandals.

But in the end Liza voluntarily stopped

the merry-go-round to seek treatment at the Betty Ford clinic. Afterwards she took time off, settling down to lead a calm existence, having friends in for cosy dinners rather than going out for a mad evening on the town.

Over the years Liza would display a continuing ill-regard for, or inability to forge, long-standing relationships with men. There were reported romances with the world-famous ballet dancer and latterly film-maker Mikhail Baryshnikov and the French singer-entertainer Charles Aznavour, whom she had first seen perform when she was seventeen. She would explain many years later that it was a turning point for her. 'I thought his act was the greatest thing I'd ever seen,' she enthused. There would also be other rumoured associations, not to mention her three marriages in 1965, 1974 and 1979. Liza would counter the lobby of disapprovers who sought to publicize what they considered was her emotional instability and immaturity by emphasizing that her problem was also that of many other women — being in love followed by disillusionment and heartbreak.

In some ways the Minnelli character is ripe for analysis, for she can be both unchanging and at the same time fickle. Her critics will point to the short, urchin-style hair which she has kept substantially unchanged for more than twenty years, and to her unyielding devotion to the popular music of a past generation. Yet to examine her career more carefully is to discover an artist who more than most has been prepared to test herself against changing times and emerging opportunities. It is hard to think of another performer of her stature who is as versatile and who now, well into her forties, could still command the highest fees for a film, a Broadway show, a cabaret performance or a TV special.

Her determination is unquestionable, yet she combines this with a keen sense of adventure. She once told *Hello* magazine: 'I'd rather risk suffering or being wrong than not try something. Security is not good for artistic types.' She added that she grew up around exceptional people like painters, musicians, writers and actors, and as a child was like a sponge . . . 'but the real struggle comes by trying to channel your impulses into something — it's important to have an objective and to pursue it with all your enthusiasm.'

But the ability to work hard can be as important as enthusiasm. Liza knows all about that and in particular the sheer agony that can result from redirecting your focus. In the late 1980s when she worked with the Pet Shop Boys on the unlikeliest of ventures which nonetheless rocketed her into the Pop Charts for the first time in her career, she admitted that the Boys worked her very hard indeed. Show business reputations and Broadway-star status count for little when redirecting your professional focus. But faced with the challenge it would have been difficult for her not to respond. 'It was a big risk for me,' she said. 'But I didn't care if it was a failure. I didn't care what people thought of it. It was just something I had to do, it helped me to find my place.'

To try to analyse the success of Liza Minnelli requires more than just a cataloguing of her skills as an actress, singer, dancer and comedienne. With some celebrities that is indeed all you get or need. But Liza is unusual if not unique in that whatever role she plays there is somehow an underlying identity with the essential Minnelli. That's not to say that she is incapable of submerging her own character and personality within a role. It is much more to do with the vision which people have, rightly or not, of the off-screen Minnelli and, as a result, of what they can accept. This kind of sub-surface understanding of her as a person in her own right leads to the supposition that it would be hard for her to be accepted as, for instance, a Calamity Jane on the one hand, or a simpering, colourless, subjugated wife on the other.

Show business has been the only occupation Liza has ever known. Performing, rehearsing, giving interviews, learning scripts and pepping up dance routines, going over songs and arrangements all are a natural way of life for her, with much of the night turned into day. She spends a lot of time in hotels or travelling from one engagement to another. At any one time she could be making a film; or performing before thousands in a vast theatre or outside venue; or working on her latest album; or moving in on a small gathering in a sophisticated nightclub with her cabaret act; or preparing her latest television spectacular. But no longer do people come to see her because she is the late Judy Garland's daughter.

It was *Time* magazine perhaps who first called her a 'dazzlingly assured and completely rounded performer, a mini-conglomerate, an entertainment monopoly'. There is no doubt that she has become one of the finest nightclub performers in the world and if she has failed to make the same kind of continuing impact in films, then perhaps it is more to do with Hollywood's inability to come up with the right material to showcase her incredible talent than with anything else.

Though undoubtedly one of the supreme stars of show business, Liza has never suffered from being encased in Hollywood's starry image. The vivid, sometimes frightening, stories from her childhood have meant that the vision of Liza

Minnelli, the ingenue, has always been hard to accept. Even when Judy was alive she was gaining the reputation of being a young lady who well knew her own mind. She has since become known as an honest and frank person not prone to flinch from the realities of life. Her failed marriages might well have dismayed her (and defeated many another), but in her own terms that is not a reason for accepting them, however painful the alternative. In press interviews her minders have sometimes warned journalists off questions about her drug and alcohol dependency and about her mother and the life she led as a child. But in reality, seldom has Liza been afraid to talk openly and candidly about such things, often taking the view that here was an opportunity to put the record straight.

As with most people, she is not anxious to rattle any personal skeletons, her own cathartic process being now well behind her, and while accepting the inevitability of those and other parts of her life, much prefers the better and brighter bits and talking about the future. She is also refreshingly honest about her appearance, and about the problems of being a star. It was near the mark when some writer said she made a good case for being vivacious rather than beautiful, after Liza had pointed out that it lessens the tensions of growing older: 'I don't think I worry about it to the degree that somebody who's once been really beautiful would,' she put it frankly. 'I worry more about my health. If I feel good, I feel I look good.' She doesn't seem to take any formal exercise and the gymnasium cult seems largely to have passed her by; but that doesn't mean she dismisses the idea of fitness. As a youngster who learned some ballet, jazz and modern dance, she was working out to a daily routine long before it became fashionable and she maintains a watch on her diet. She told *Harper's Bazaar* in 1988: 'I enjoy Japanese and Italian cuisines, but once a month I just gotta have a pot roast.' She is said to adore cream cheese and sour cream on nearly everything, along with Japanese and French foods.

Her honesty sometimes rebounds on

her own kind. She has little in common with actors and singers who make vast sums of money yet are constantly complaining about the stresses and the way their life isn't their own any more. Nor does she align with the other extreme where celebrities seem to relish the idea of robbing the punters to line their own pockets, being paid enormous fees while at the same time glibly boasting 'It's better than working for a living.'

Liza has a more balanced judgement, as expressed to *Photoplay* more than twenty years ago: 'It's great, but sometimes I can't believe how much money they're paying me for doing this. It seems like so much for doing so little. There are other times though, when I feel I just can't give any more, when I think they couldn't pay me enough.' She said the time to watch out was when it wasn't fun any more. 'Some people take their success so seriously that it makes me crazy,' she added. 'They say their life isn't their own and that people are always bothering them, but listen . . . it's everything they've always wanted.'

She never gives the impression of being a sham. She is open, frank, might well have controversial or extreme views and will state them clearly. Yet she never seems to set out deliberately to insult or hurt. Nor would she shock simply to gain attention, score a point or make a cheap buck. What she says you feel instinctively is genuine; she's not taking you for a ride. Whether you like her or not as a person or a celebrity — you may profoundly disagree with much of what she says or does — the over-riding impression is that she is open and honest and would not parade her star status or put you down to make a statement in which she didn't fully believe.

In a sense Liza Minnelli has never gone out of fashion. She works constantly and never seems to run out of energy or audiences. Every Minnelli concert is an event. She has, however, a shrewd working knowledge of her own limitations in terms of popular appeal as well as her strengths, so she astutely spaces out her dates. For one thing she doesn't need the money any more. But more important, in so doing she knows it is difficult for anyone to get too much of Liza Minnelli. She likes to feel that they'll come back for more. So far they always have.

8

New York, New York — Her Kind of Town

IT isn't easy to pinpoint the reasons for Liza's prolonged absence from the big screen after *Cabaret*. You could say that she was too busy and too successful giving concerts to make space for another picture. And after *Cabaret* it is likely that she would be looking for another musical to give her the best chance of a similar triumph. Liza herself has said that following *Cabaret* producers and agents bombarded her with scripts. 'They came flooding in by mail and special delivery, but I read them all and tossed them aside,' she added.

One she should have tossed aside was *Lucky Lady*, which though full of promise turned out to be a disaster. Perhaps, since few films were being made with strong female leads, Liza simply ran out of patience and, after three years looking for a good part, finally gave in and took what was on offer. At least theoretically *Lucky Lady* gave her the opportunity of a strong leading role alongside major co-stars Burt Reynolds and Gene Hackman. Director Stanley Donen, whose talents along with those of Gene Kelly brought a refreshing new vitality to the Hollywood musical in the late 1940s and early 1950s, said Liza was the first person he thought of after reading the script: 'I sent it to her, she liked it, and of course I was delighted.' Donen told *Films and Filming* at the time: 'Two years ago Liza said to me: "Let's find a movie to do together" and I had agreed, so when this script came up I wrote saying "Dear Liza, I think you'll like this", and she read it that day and said "I'll do it. You're absolutely right".'

The only tenuous similarity with *Cabaret* was that Liza would play a former cabaret girl but this time it was set in 1930 Tijuana where she joined up with a couple of adventurers smuggling liquor into the United States. The action takes place during America's Prohibition era with

Claire (Liza), Walker (Burt Reynolds) and Kibby (Gene Hackman) using the sloop, Lucky Lady, for a rum-running service in a get-rich-quick scheme. They relish the danger, excitement and the fun of it all. Liza played what *Photoplay* described as the 'undisputed queen of the blockade runners, the tough-talking, hard-loving mistress of Lucky Lady'.

This background of high adventure and rousing action aside, the film also tells a more personal story, with the three stars finding their way to a perfect relationship and a new way of life. Donen was impressed with Liza's high work rate on the movie and the way she would consult him about many of the scenes and how they should be handled. 'Everything she does is with a great deal of thought and preparation,' he commented at the time. With three major box office names fronting the picture, and with screenplay by Willard Huyck and Gloria Katz, *Lucky Lady* was tipped to be one of the major releases of 1975. Billed as a period adventure, and filmed largely at a remote location in Mexico, the picture developed plenty of action including an attack on the law-breakers by air and naval forces and battle scenes between the coast guard and the blockade runners. But, alas, even all this failed to salvage the picture from humiliating reviews and lukewarm public appeal. Reviewed the *New Yorker*: 'They're all rum runners in the early 1930s and they're all meant to be adorable. This is a big, expensive movie for people who don't mind being treated like hicks: the audience is expected to shudder with delight every time it hears an obscenity or sees a big movie star grin.' It is hard to believe from its dismal showing at the box office that Huyck and Katz, who had scored heavily with their *American Graffiti*, were paid a reported $400,000 for the scenario. The best that Liza could hope for was that the ridiculous red wig she was called upon to wear for her role would provide sufficient disguise to help her forget the picture almost as soon as it was finished. Three-quarters through the movie one of the characters looks to the others and says: 'I know we're doing something wrong, but I can't figure out what it is.' Most audiences could have told him — *making the film in the first place*. Or spending huge sums of money in re-shooting the ending — the original idea, which had the stars, Lucky Lady and its contraband cargo, blown sky-high, would seem to have been a more appropriate finale given the circumstances. That would have been one way for them to escape the ignominy.

In less than a year Liza seemed to be on firmer ground when she decided to team with her father in *A Matter of Time*, but again the results were miserably disappointing. At the start the picture seemed to hold out a lot of promise, for this was to be the manifestation of Vincente's long-held vision of bringing *Carmella* to the screen, though it had gone through *The Film of Memory* and *Nina* before ending up as *A Matter of Time*. Vincente Minnelli, not normally given to extravagant claims, said that *A Matter of Time* was a touching, exciting, heart-warming story with a lot of comedy. 'For ten years I've had my eye on this property,' he said, 'but the movie rights didn't become available until

1973. When they did my partners and I quickly snapped them up. When I first read Maurice Druon's novel on which the script is based, I felt it would make a marvellous picture.'

Liza too was excited. She explained: 'When my father sent me the script of *A Matter of Time* it had me hooked from the start. Excitedly, I said to him: "Come on, let's make it. Let's make it together".'

Other major pointers to success were Liza's big-name co-stars Ingrid Bergman and Charles Boyer and the galaxy of Oscar winners being paraded for the film. For in addition to Liza's Oscar for *Cabaret*, Miss Bergman had won an Academy Award for earlier work; so too had the film's British director of photography, Geoffrey Unsworth, who had worked with Liza on *Cabaret* and *Lucky Lady*.

Liza was obviously attracted to *A Matter of Time* because it was about two women — the first time, she reckoned, that a production of such quality had been based on two actresses and not a male performer like Redford, Newman or Brando. 'It should be a film to delight women's libbers,' she explained. But somehow the special chemistry which should have resulted from the individual talents of father and daughter being brought together wasn't apparent. This was a rather lame tale about Nina (played by Liza), a simple Italian country chambermaid working in a third rate hotel in Rome, whose imagination is so stirred by the stories of an impoverished but once famous and now elderly Contessa (played by Ingrid Bergman), that she begins to fantasize about incidents in the Contessa's fabulous past, with herself in the role. Gradually, she undergoes a metamorphosis that completely transforms her in outlook, manner and appearance.

Much of the movie was shot in Italy and Liza loved some of the extravagant and extraordinary gowns she had to wear. She told *Film Review*: 'They're all pretty eye-catching, but two in particular are quite stunning. One is a white satin creation with black lace, topped by a hat with three birds of paradise on it. This outfit is my own favourite. The other is a gold dress which I wear in the magnificent fancy-dress ball scenes in Venice.' There was also music in the film. During the Venice ball scenes, Liza joins with the orchestra in singing George Gershwin's 'Do it Again', but this and two other numbers specially written for Liza by John Kander and Fred Ebb — the title song and 'The Me I Haven't Met Yet' — were not enough to save the picture. *Halliwell's Film Guide* assessment told a dismal story — 'Interminable even in its abbreviated form, this woebegone fantasy is a tribute to his miscast daughter by a director who never had much sense of plot to begin with. It has to be seen to be believed.'

MGM had originally bought the rights to the book, before Vincente acquired them, but never made the film. Securing Bergman and Boyer to co-star with Liza, though both were long since past their peak, seemed like good casting. The film took fourteen weeks to make, but never got off the ground. It had little success in America and was never shown in either Britain or France. As Kathleen Carrol in *The Movie* suggests ' . . . once made it would have been kinder never to have released this hilariously inept, painfully old-fashioned movie.' Years after, Liza would still find the memories of *A Matter of Time* depressing, hinting that some of the blame for its failure was down to the decision by American International Pictures to take control away from her father in the final stages. It did appear, however, that Vincente's work was not matching his reputation, probably because he was unwell; and once AIP saw what he had produced, they decided on significant re-editing. Frustrated, perhaps a little angry, and certainly worried about her father, Liza was moved to organize a full-page advertisement in the Hollywood trade press, with the endorsements of a number of the film industry's creative people, including Martin Scorsese, protesting at AIP's action.

Liza, however, was left with some happy memories of working with her father and the consolation that *A Matter of Time* had been more physically comfortable for her in the making than *Lucky Lady*. She said that in the latter, during shooting in Mexico, there had been nearly fifty people jammed together for twelve hours a day, week in and week out, on a 63–foot racing ketch, including a crew of eight and twenty-five key technicians. 'It was sheer murder,' was her verdict.

The accumulated failure of *Lucky Lady* and *A Matter of Time* was depressing and disheartening for Liza, who by this time may have been wondering if it would not be better to forget about Hollywood altogether. In the meantime she continued with personal appearances where her reputation was untarnished and where, being herself, audiences could easily see and appreciate the energy, the personality and the singing and dancing talent of Liza Minnelli, the supreme performer. Only Streisand perhaps could have been so dynamic in front of a live audience, but by this time she was making no secret of her dislike of live concerts and personal appearances and giving almost all of her time to films and recordings.

In 1976 Liza did make a brief return to the movies appearing as herself, as did a number of other star names including Anne Bancroft, Burt Reynolds, Paul Newman and James Caan, in a panel of guest stars in the novel and extraordinary Mel Brooks picture *Silent Movie*. This spoof story, also by Brooks, about an alcoholic producer who thinks a silent movie in an age of talkies and technicolour enough of a novelty to be a runaway success, included Britain's zany Marty Feldman, along with Bernadette Peters and Sid Caesar, in the cast list. Marcel Marceau would go down in history as the only person to utter a word in this 87–minute novelty. The word? 'Non'!

But if her film record could have been more inspiring, in the 1970s Liza had continued to attract the attention of the record companies. 'Come Saturday Morning', which had been the theme tune from her film *The Sterile Cuckoo (Pookie)*, had been released by A & M in April 1970 and combined some popular favourites like 'Nevertheless', 'Love Story', 'Didn't We', 'Leaving on a Jet Plane' and 'On a Slow Boat to China' with the less enduring 'Raggedy Ann and Raggedy Andy', 'Wailing of the Willow',

'Wherefore and Why', 'Don't Let Me Lose This Dream', 'Simon', 'MacArthur Park' and the title song.

In December of that same year in the United States, and in Britain in April 1972, A & M released a string of popular all-time favourites under the title *New Feelin'*. This LP comprised 'Love For Sale', the old Lena Horne number 'Stormy Weather', 'Come Rain or Shine', 'Lazy Bones', 'Can't Help Loving That Man of Mine', '(I Wonder Where My) Easy Rider's Gone', 'The Man I Love', 'How Long Has This Been Going On', 'God Bless the Child' and 'Maybe This Time'. This popular album offering was followed by the sound track recording from *Cabaret*, released in the United States in April 1972 and in the UK the following month. Liza sang as solos 'Mein Herr', 'Maybe This Time', and 'Cabaret'. She shared 'Money, Money, Money' with Joel Grey. Joel Grey performed 'If You Could See Her', 'Willkommen' and 'Two Ladies'.

Liza Minnelli 'Live' at the Olympia was also released during 1972 in both the United States and Britain, with *Liza*

With a Z(ee), from the sound track of her television show, coming out in November 1972 in the US and in March 1973 in the UK. *The Liza Minnelli Foursider* followed in February 1973 (released in Britain with some changes in August 1973 as Portrait of Liza). It was in 1973 that Liza moved to CBS and her first offering from her new label was *The Singer*, released in both the United States and Britain in May that year. Of the twelve tracks the following were probably the most well known: 'You're So Vain', 'Where is the Love' and 'You are the Sunshine of My Life'.

It was also in 1973 that Liza astounded her followers by courageously recording some back-up vocals on two selections of an Alice Cooper album, 'Teenage Lament '74' and 'Man With Golden Gun'. *Liza at the Winter Garden* was released in Britain (May 1973) and in the United States (May 1974) and included 'If You Could Read My Mind', 'Come Back to Me', 'Shine On Harvest Moon', 'Exactly Like You', 'More Than You Know', 'I Can See Clearly Now' and 'You Made Me Love You'. It was perhaps a vintage period for Liza Minnelli on record and, together with her live dates, must have gone a long way towards making up for any disappointments she felt about the dismal progress of her film career.

For a time also, her marriage to Jack Haley Jnr offered some compensation, and confounded the cynics by remaining intact. His basic intelligence and sound ambitions had set him well on the way to a successful business career, and he ultimately became head of 20th Century Fox's television division. The marriage seemed sound enough when Liza was working on *Lucky Lady*, for he made regular trips to Mexico to see her. Her high spirits and excitable nature benefited from Haley's calming influence and the security he seemed to bring to the marriage. After their wedding they had settled into a new home and even talked confidentially about having a family. Liza was always happiest when kept busy and at about this time she did a TV spectacular called *Life Goes to the Movies*, based on the way *Life* magazine had covered the history of the movies over the years. She played a cameo role as one of a number of celebrities chosen to introduce segments of the presentation, similar to her role in the earlier *That's Entertainment*. She even went back to Broadway for a five-week stint in August 1975 taking over the lead as replacement for her old friend Gwen Verdon, the star of *Chicago*, when she needed an operation on her throat. Curiously, the film version of *Chicago* would surface periodically over a number of years as a potential project for Liza, who saw herself in the role of Roxie Hart, but it never happened.

Liza could virtually name her own price for restaurant, night club and theatre appearances, but she confessed at one point that she didn't want to be a cabaret artist all her life. She was delighted when the chance came for her to make another picture and quietly thrilled that it was to be a musical. In 1976 when shooting began on the movie, the large scale, uncompromising Hollywood musical had been succeeded by the musical drama, of which *Cabaret* had been the supreme example, especially for Liza.

New York, New York would follow in that tradition, the expertise of Italian American director Martin Scorsese, one of the film industry's major creative talents, applied with telling effect on an $8½ million homage to the big band era of the Forties. It promised to be an exciting project with Liza securing a plum role. The idea for New York, New York was to start with producers Robert Chartoff and Irwin Winkler, already a formidable team in having recently seen their film Rocky gain an Academy Award. The story goes that Sylvester Stallone had gone to Chartoff and Winkler with the idea for Rocky and the two of them then encouraged him to write it. They also gave their support to his idea to star in it, further demonstrating their faith in the picture by agreeing to underwrite the costs of any over-run on the budget, allowing United Artists to finally agree the deal.

Both Chartoff and Winkler were staunch enthusiasts of the Forties style of big band music and intended to make a love story set against the pulsating beat and exciting noise of this musical period.

Blues in the Night had always been one of Winkler's favourite movies. Probably as a result of their generous optimism over *Rocky* — which was to be fully justified by the picture's phenomenal success — they managed to interest United Artists again in their latest project. But their excitement about the new movie could so easily have sucked them into a cloying morass of nostalgia and little else. On the other hand, cleverly handled with sensitivity and discretion, there was just a sneaking chance that it could turn out to be one of the best pictures of the year. In the end it finished up somewhere between. Liza takes the part of Francine Evans, a band singer, with co-star Robert De Niro, one of Hollywood's best young actors, playing Jimmy Doyle, a talented tenor saxophone player. There is a spectacular opening sequence which, following scenes of wild celebration in Times Square in New York on VJ Day 1945, depicts a packed Starlight Terrace ballroom of the Waldorf Astoria also heavily into celebrating. Dancers are jiving and swinging to the big band sound in a frenzy of good-natured, chaotic and wildly enthusiastic delight that the war is over.

It is during these celebrations that Francine and Jimmy first meet. Jimmy is brash and arrogant, gum-chewing and irritatingly insistent in his multi-coloured Hawaiian shirt and civilian trousers, his forces uniform already discarded. He doesn't have a date and becomes a continuing nuisance to Francine, who proves more than a match for him, continually saying 'no' and pushing him away. As the official synopsis explained: 'She is sitting alone at a ringside table near Tommy Dorsey and his band (with William Tole a convincing TD lookalike), still in the WAC uniform in which she had been entertaining the troops, while her girl friend Ellen (Kathi McGinnis) is on the dance floor locked in the arms of Jimmy's wartime buddy, Eddie di Muzio (Frank Silvera). As Jimmy moves in for the kill, Francine proves she has a technique in witty rebuffs which is more than equal to his non-stop barrage of verbal thrusts.'

From there on there is little which is original, or even novel, about the story.

Jimmy and Francine grow closer together and are signed up together with a band at the relatively seedy Palm Club, Jimmy joining the sax section and Francine as featured vocalist. They celebrate together and are seen to become more attracted to each other, but almost immediately Francine receives the offer of a bigger job touring with the band of Frankie Harte (played by real-life saxophonist Georgie Auld). She feels she cannot afford to turn the offer down, but leaves a message for Jimmy. He is angry and his pride has been hurt. He packs in his job with the band and takes off in pursuit.

When he finally catches up with Francine he manages to convince her of their love for each other and through her influence he gets a job with Harte's band. He pursues her relentlessly, smothering her with kisses, writing a song for her, and eventually takes her off in her nightdress before the Justice of the Peace for them to become man and wife.

But the popularity of the big bands is fading and Frankie Harte tells Francine that he will have to break up the band. Secretly, Francine persuades Frankie to let Jimmy take over the band. He begins to introduce his own brand of advanced modern music into their repertoire, but refuses to acknowledge that it is really Francine's singing which is keeping the punters happy. Jimmy does not share Francine's joy when she tells him she is pregnant and in the awkward relationship which follows, she returns to New York to await the birth. Jimmy replaces her with a third-rate singer and soon realizes through the thinning attendances at their dances that it was Francine's popularity as a singer which was keeping the band together.

There are various emotional dramas which culminate in a showdown argument which precipitates the birth of their baby and the end of their marriage. Francine goes on to bigger and better things, becoming a major recording artist and finally securing the lead in a spectacular Hollywood musical, *Happy Endings*. Jimmy opens his own jazz nightspot called the Harlem Club with his be-bop friends. Ten years after their first meeting Francine returns to the Starlight Terrace of the Waldorf Astoria as a star attraction. Jimmy listens to her acclaimed performance of 'New York, New York' which he had composed for her when they toured together, and is moved to seek a reconciliation. As the official synopsis has it: 'Francine too is tempted to accept his invitation to a reunion meeting but she knows instinctively that she would be crazy to break up the peaceful domestic triangle she has formed with pianist Paul Wilson, played by Barry Primus, who took over the band after Jimmy's walkout, and her young son. Although she knows she will always have a place for Jimmy in her heart, Francine feels that a love story is like a song . . . it is beautiful while it lasts.'

It was obvious that Scorsese hadn't set out to make just another musical drama. He classified it as 'a dark musical about careers and artistic drives'. Even so, followers of big-band music would form the greatest section of its audience and would not be disappointed. Great and abiding memories of the swing era were brought vividly to life as more than twenty top hits first made famous by the bands of Glenn Miller, Benny Goodman, Tommy and Jimmy Dorsey were featured. Included in this swingtime extravaganza were 'The More We Know', 'Do Nothing 'Til You Hear From Me', 'Honeysuckle Rose', 'Pennsylvania Six Five Thousand', 'I'm Getting Sentimental Over You' and a excellent long, long sequence of 'Opus One', originally made famous by the Tommy Dorsey Orchestra when the record was selected as the theme for the Allied Expeditionary Forces radio record programme, *Duffle Bag*, following the opening of the Second Front in 1944.

Liza could indulge in a selection of fine tunes including a superb interpretation of 'The Man I Love', a few delightful bars of 'Once in a While' and 'Taking a Chance on Love', 'You Are My Lucky Star', and a revealing 'You Brought a New Kind of Love to Me'. The last of these was used as a brief yet musically inspiring showcase for Liza's vocal talent and Auld's superb tenor-sax-playing as Jimmy and Francine audition 'as a boy-and-girl' act in the early part of the film. George Auld, a noted saxophone player by profession, whose roots go back to the era of swinging bands when he played for the original Benny Goodman and Artie Shaw orchestras, carefully coached De Niro, helping him with the correct handling and fingering of the instrument.

The picture made the news for its dazzling cinematography and many comic scenes, some of which by today's standards are over-long and tedious, as well as for its upbeat musical numbers. But it lost its way, according to Ronald Bergan in *The United Artists Story*, when the original four-hour movie was cut down to 153 minutes and then 137 minutes on general release, taking with it many of the minor characters. The narrative was weakened and some continuity lost, but as Bergan concluded: 'Despite this, however, it was an entertaining pastiche of Forties musicals, Minnelli and De Niro were a redoubtable duo and there were some vigorous set pieces from director Scorsese . . . ' The spectacularly successful all-music, all-dancing finale is in the very best traditions of the Hollywood musical, a classic triumph of its kind. Certainly, as time went on, it would be remembered for Liza's authentic interpretive skills as an actress, as well as a musical performer.

It was probably the film Liza most enjoyed making. She said at the time: 'It's not quite like anything I've ever seen,' and told Tom Oliver of *Photoplay*: 'For five months I worked from seven in the morning until 11 at night on that movie. We'd arrive at the studio in the morning, write out a scene, then do it . . . I can't remember ever sitting down.' The screenplay was by Mardik Martin and Earl Mac Rauch from the latter's original story, but so much of the film was improvised that Liza said she ended up being more herself than in any other role she had ever played.

Whether or not the film itself stirred memories for Liza, the process of making it certainly did. For although the movie was called *New York, New York*, the film was shot in what remained of the old Culver City studios, near Hollywood, which MGM had built as long ago as 1915. She actually occupied her mother's old dressing room and much of the picture was filmed on stage 29, where many of the vintage musicals from more than thirty years before were shot, including Judy's *The Wizard of Oz*. Vincente had also produced many of his earlier successes in the same studios. In the picture Liza has more than 50 costume changes, including a WAC uniform, and looks authentic Forties with cherry red lipstick and a Syd Guilaroff hairdo. The schedule, said Liza, was 'excruciating, exhilarating and what came out of it is really interesting with a lot of good music'.

Music certainly was vital and Liza's now long-time musical associates Fred Ebb and John Kander produced four new songs for the film, including 'Happy Endings', which *Film Review* described as 'a spectacular production number'. Others were 'But the World Goes Round', 'There Goes the Ball Game' and the 'Theme from *New York, New York*'. But it was Liza's interpretation of the title song which she delivered with such panache, spirit and zest which was the unqualified hit, even if finally the film fell short of its promise. This Fred Fob and John Kander composition in popular memory and appeal eclipsed a different song with the same name from the film *On the Town* almost thirty years before, and was to become as closely associated with Liza as *Cabaret* and *Liza With a Z*, despite Sinatra's later challenge. London was chosen to host the European Premiere of *New York, New York*. The occasion received royal distinction when Her Royal Highness Princess Margaret agreed to attend the charity performance, in aid of the St John Ambulance Centenary, at the Odeon, Leicester Square on 15 September 1977.

New York, New York would not be a major triumph for Liza in the style of *Cabaret*, even though with the passing of time the film has been seen to deserve a higher rating than it achieved at the time of its release, if only for its musical content. Despite that, and although Robert De Niro had already gained an Oscar for his part in *The Godfather Part 2*, there was little doubt that Liza was the picture's unequivocal star. Even the film's most severe critics singled her out for praise: ' . . . Minnelli's performance as a band singer was its only redeeming feature,' assesses David

Shipman in his *The Great Movie Stars*. Time would confirm it, though, as second to *Cabaret* in public recognition and appreciation of Liza's talent, even if there was little to commend other than her polished and professional performance.

At a more personal level Liza's outgoing attitude to life meant that her attraction to men led her enthusiastically and easily into new relationships, and it didn't really shock anyone when rumours of an affair between her and Scorsese began circulating, but Liza strongly denied that there was anything between them. She stated that her marriage to Jack Haley Jnr was strong, and put the stories down to Hollywood's insatiable appetite for gossip. Even so, her marriage was to prove unendurable and in January 1978, while starring on Broadway as Michelle Craig in *The Act*, she and Haley separated and agreed to live apart. Six months later her marriage was officially at an end, although her divorce would not be final until April 1979; but within eight months she would marry for a third time. She had met Mark Gero, a handsome 27-year-old Italian, when he was a stage manager for *The Act* and the couple had fallen in love during the run of the show. They had been seen together at the trendy Studio 54 in January 1979, but had denied rumours that they planned to marry. Mark was keen for them to marry, but Liza at first resisted, perhaps because she was disillusioned with marriage; in any event, it was not long since her divorce from Haley. But when she found that she was pregnant she was prepared for marriage, and the wedding took place on 4 December 1979 at St Bartholomew's Episcopal Church in New York City, with a ceremony conducted by the Rev Peter Delaney. Lorna Luft was Liza's Matron of Honour and the twenty-plus guests included Elizabeth Taylor and Fred Ebb. The reception was held at the home of fashion guru Halston, one of the in-crowd of Liza's up-tempo friends of the period, on East 63rd Street in New York.

Liza's third marriage would have its turbulent times but had the substance and resilience to last for more than ten years. She would be happily pregnant three times, but all were destined to end traumatically in miscarriages. Having no children has been one of life's greatest disappointments for her. But now she is philosophical about the way things work out. Having stated earlier that no home is complete without a child, she said more recently: 'If you can't have kids, that's one of the realities you have to deal with.'

There were other realities which Liza would be driven to handle at the time. Her growing habit of taking Valium and other pills would have to be contained and her alcohol intake was destined to present problems. Those close enough to know might well have wondered if Liza was beginning to follow a parallel pattern to Judy, for towards the end of the 1970s she did not give self-care much of a priority. Alongside her drink and drug dependency she continued to smoke heavily in order to ease the stress of life in the fast lane of show business. 'People who sit in their rooms dreaming of being on the stage or making a record have no idea what it's like,' she once said. 'Nothing can prepare you for what it does for your privacy. You can't let your life be ruined by it. Some people in this business have been driven bananas by it.'

In the meantime though, she was kept busy enough appearing in person in *The Act* (previously titled *Shine it On*), with songs Kander and Ebb had written specially for her. Housed on West 44th Street at the Majestic Theatre, the musical opened in New York in October 1977 after earlier runs in Chicago and San Francisco. Co-starring with Barry Nelson, Liza played a once-famous Hollywood star trying for a come-back at Las Vegas, and in some respects it turned out to be a surprising jewel in Liza's show business crown. Despite what some critics said about the play, Liza continued to be an enormous personal draw. The earlier run in San Francisco had been a sell-out, and after it opened in Los Angeles on 30 August 1977 Gower Champion replaced Martin Scorsese as director. When the show opened on Broadway at the Majestic Theatre on 30 October, the box office had been a sell-out for months ahead, despite what had previously been considered almost prohibitive seat prices. Liza received rave notices and was even crowned 'Miss Ziegfeld'. Her New Year's Eve performance created a record, bringing in more money from that single performance than any other show had done in one night in the history of Broadway. London's Keith Jarvis, a committed Minnelli fan, was in the United States at the time and managed to get a ticket for *The Act*. 'She was great in it,' he said, 'despite being up and down with illness and going through the drug problem. She was in it for ten months and she was 'the whole show' — a very demanding part.' She had already collapsed during an out-of-town performance and, after the show had opened in New York, she was taken to hospital suffering once more from exhaustion. Once she began to feel better and, disobeying doctor's orders, had returned to the show, a fire in her apartment — rumoured to have been caused by her smoking in bed — put her back in hospital for treatment for smoke inhalation and a lung infection. Her indifferent health and this misadventure meant that she would miss quite a number of performances of *The Act*, and in November 1977 Liza was forced to rest for three weeks through illness, but her portrayal of an almost type-cast role, in a play which was built around a nightclub act, was enough to bring her another Tony Award.

If Liza was having difficulty in finding a film project to pin her talents to, she still managed to be about the most ubiquitous performer around at this time. She took the remaining years of the decade like a stallion hurtling towards the winning post in the Grand National. She rested briefly after *The Act* closed and then embarked on a gruelling international tour with dancers Roger Minami from *The Act* and Obba Babatunde. Between 1 September and 18 December 1978 she played almost a dozen areas in the United States, as well as Canada, Denmark, Germany, Sweden, Switzerland, Belgium, Holland, England and France, with a popular musical programme which stretched almost the full length and breadth of her extensive repertoire; from 'How Long Has This Been Going On?' to a 'New York Medley', 'Someone to Watch Over Me' to 'Happy Anniversary', 'London Town' to 'Cabaret' and 'You Do Something to Me'. It was in December that she was in Europe with key dates at the Palladium and the Olympia in Paris; in September she found time to receive the Canadian Variety Club Award; and while in France she taped the TV presentation, *Liza in Rehearsal*.

It was early in 1979 that she appeared briefly and temporarily as Lillian Hellman in the off-Broadway production about the McCarthy period, *Are You Now or Have You Ever Been?*, produced by Frank Gero, Mark's father. In February 1979 she was on tour again, this time visiting Brazil, Florida, Georgia, Rhode Island, Ohio, Nevada, Missouri, Texas and Canada, with her last appearance in Montreal on 24 June. She then flew to Los Angeles to star in a tribute presentation to Dr S. Wile of the Reiss Davis Child Study Center, which was held in the International Ballroom of the Beverly Hilton Hotel on 27 June. She was back in England on 23 July for The Martha Graham Dance Company ballet presentation of *The Owl and the Pussycat* at Covent Garden. Liza narrated the Edward Lear poem on which the ballet is based and took delight in being presented to Princess Alexandra. Liza had given a similar presentation at the Lincoln Center's Metropolitan Opera House in Washington on 26 June 1978, also with The Martha Graham Dance Company. In August there was a flying visit to Berlin, and in September she was back in New York for the Jerry Lewis Labor Day Telethon. That same month witnessed her enormous success at Carnegie Hall (4 to 14 September), after which, between 18 September and 1 October, she taped the TV special, *Goldie and Liza Together*, with Goldie Hawn at Hollywood's ABC studios. She was then on the road once more from 4 October to 25 November with an 'all tickets sold' tour. It seemed even at this stage in her career that she would be known, and most of all become remembered, as a concert performer. For despite her enormously high profile as an entertainer and an outstanding international celebrity, she had only made one truly memorable picture in more than ten years.

It was probably that very fact which

panicked her into appearing in the upcoming Dudley Moore picture, *Arthur*, made in 1980. Her secondary billing was in one sense an insult to her talent and stature as an international superstar. But her role as the kooky, out-of-work actress Linda Marolla with whom Arthur (Moore) falls helplessly in love after seeing her shoplifting from a posh store, wasn't big enough to warrant greater acknowledgement. In any event it was the film which attracted her. She wasn't too much bothered about the relatively low billing; she was just delighted to be once more in front of the cameras. In the end the picture's success would help to sharpen her film profile.

Liza admitted at about the time *Arthur* was being released that she didn't see her future clearly, but said she would never stop singing for live audiences. 'But I know that, like Mama, my future lies primarily in motion pictures,' she added. Pushing the film at release time she said that she was sure *Arthur* would do well. 'It's a funny, charming story, and perhaps the public prefers me paired with Englishmen' (Sir John Gielgud was also in the picture). 'I just loved working with Dudley. He lifted my spirits and this is his best work since *10*.' It was with *10* that Dudley Moore became an overnight sensation in pictures and in the end he wouldn't do too badly with *Arthur* either. For it was reported that on the strength of *Arthur*'s success, Dud was offered $3 million (1981 values, remember) for his next screen comedy. Liza went on: 'I want to do more comedy, and musicals too, but the market for musicals is underestimated by producers, and something like *Cabaret*, which blends music, acting and biting social comment, is extremely rare.'

In *Arthur*, Dudley plays the world's richest and most lovable drunk, Arthur Bach, a millionaire with a sparkling sense of humour and an impending $750 million inheritance if he marries beautiful heiress Susan Johnson, played by Jill Eikenberry. The only problems seem to be that he loves drink a lot and doesn't love Susan at all. This dilemma, which forces *Arthur* into moderating his lifestyle, is the basis of a storyline which is paper thin, but whose characters were colourful enough to earn *Arthur* the distinction at one time of being the most popular film in America and the year's funniest movie. Sir John Gielgud, as Arthur's valet Hobson, produced a meritorious performance of dry acerbic wit sufficient for *Film Review* to decide: 'If Gielgud was ever born to a role, this is it.' By keen critical standards it was not a good picture, but as was pointed out by one critic, it was a sign of the times that it made a lot of money; it grossed over £60 million at the box office. It must have been particularly frustrating for Liza that, despite its outstanding commercial success and its distinctions (an Oscar for Gielgud and an Oscar nomination for Moore) the picture did little to advance her own Hollywood career.

Full of hope about *Arthur*, Liza confessed: 'I can't afford many more poor choices. I hate to be commercial, and I'm not about to cop out and do trash, nude scenes or awful-but-popular pictures, but I want a hit.' It was the first time she had worked with Gielgud, but looking back to the making of the picture some twenty years later in 1993,

Sir John told me: 'I never had the chance to know Liza Minnelli at all well, and can only say that she was the most enchanting and professional colleague and it was the greatest pleasure working with her. When she had already finished her own scenes she took the trouble to come all the way back to the studio, to bring me a present and wish me well in shooting my own scenes.' Sir John went on: 'She is incredibly versatile and gifted and I learned much from watching her. She is quite without star tantrums or the expectation of privileges, a real star both on and off the set.'

Anyone who appreciates talent had to sympathize and share Liza's urgent hope for another Minnelli hit, for on a personal level life had been cruel to her of late. Soon after her wedding to Mark Gero she had been taken to hospital in New York with severe abdominal pains, the preliminary to a traumatic miscarriage. Now in her mid-thirties she seemed desperate to have a child, though there had been talk of gynaecological problems which would make childbirth difficult. She put it out of her mind and tried instead to focus strongly on her career, but some months later, on the verge of a nationwide tour with her *Cabaret* co-star Joel Grey, she suffered more stomach pain and was taken into hospital in Boston where she was found to be two months pregnant. The medics said that with rest they thought everything would be fine. She rested, but again she miscarried. Mentally devastated, she was able to regain some of her traditional sparkle when she and Joel finally embarked on the postponed tour. Predictably, the tour was an outstanding success and, according to Michael Freedland in *Liza With a Z*: 'Everybody who was anybody in town came (to the Los Angeles open-air Greek Theatre). Frank Sinatra sent her a note saying: "You were wonderful, absolutely sensational, and I realize I'm getting too old to sing 'New York, New York'. I loved you, but you moved around too much on the stage. Love, Uncle Frank".'

There was to be a third miscarriage, and when *Hello* magazine asked her some years later, on the eve of her tenth wedding anniversary while she was appearing in Madrid, if she would still like to have children she replied: 'I would love to have children. Of course it's all in God's hands — perhaps I should ask my mother in heaven for some help on the subject!' Though, as far as can be judged, she has never seriously contemplated adoption.

Professionally, at concerts Liza could do no wrong. Her fans turned out in their thousands. No-one made a greater impression, a stronger impact before a live audience. But despite her remarkable success and huge financial reward from her concert performances, the 1980s would not start at all well for Liza. *Arthur* was released in 1981 and, despite everything, would turn out to be about the best thing she would do in the next five or so years, excluding her concerts. Much of her other stuff was low key and reports of various interesting possibilities just didn't seem to turn out. In 1982 she decided to take almost a year off in an attempt to overcome her gynaecological problems, but embarked on a hectic concert programme in 1983. She demonstrated her sincere love and affection for her father when she sang her heart out at a special show to mark Vincente's seventy-third birthday. Then there was the stage presentation of *The Rink*, in which she played Chita Rivera's daughter, but again Liza was playing a secondary role, even though Kander and Ebb had penned a special score. It was early in 1984 that she had to leave the show temporarily to have a benign lump removed from her neck. She left the show permanently in late July after about six months. A more tempting possibility was a part in *Gypsy*, but the idea never saw the light of day.

Meanwhile, her lifestyle was not helping her physical and mental condition. She drove herself hard with little sleep, living off her reserves of emotional and nervous energy. Her life with Mark was known to have survived its turbulent times. A few years later she would look back on these times with almost nightmarish horror. 'I hated my thirties,' she would recall. 'Well, my thirties were great until I was thirty-five and then I became CD, chemically dependent. Alcoholic. I had the disease, and that made me so tired I didn't appreciate life at all.' There were many days she just didn't want to get out of bed. She got it fixed so strongly in her mind that she had leukaemia that she confessed to having been actually relieved when told that she had a clinical disease of drug and alcohol addiction. In 1983 there was the insignificant *The King of Comedy*, to be followed a year later by the equally pedestrian, in career terms, *The Muppets Take Manhattan*.

It was in 1984, within a few days of pulling out of *The Rink*, that she courageously admitted she needed help and checked into the Betty Ford Centre in Rancho Mirage, California.

9

Conquest at Carnegie Hall

THE news that Liza Minnelli had checked into the Betty Ford Clinic sent shock waves around her community of fans. What they feared most, that she had significant drink and drug problems, had been substantiated. Uncommitted members of the general public saw it as just another pampered, over-rich and undisciplined celebrity who couldn't handle the good life. It gave sections of the press a bonus chance to drag out recollections of Judy and the old 'like mother, like daughter' syndrome.

But her close friends and associates, though sympathetic, were hardly surprised. Half-sister Lorna had strongly encouraged her to go for treatment. Her friend, Elizabeth Taylor, had recognized the signs. It would have been more surprising to those who knew her best, had she not fallen victim to drug and drink abuse.

Over nearly twenty years, the taking of calming Valium, booze, and what she called party drugs to make her feel good, had steadily grown into an addiction.

She has never blamed her emotionally-charged childhood for any of this, but growing up in a home environment where it was normal to take tablets to get to sleep, to keep going, to ease black moods of depression and calm pinnacles of excitability, can't have helped. She was introduced to amphetamines as a puppy-fat teenager wanting to lose weight to advance her career. It's not difficult to move on from there. As she admitted at a time of soul-baring a few years ago: 'I didn't take my first Valium thinking, "Hey, I want to be an addict". I never had a self-destructive bone in my body, though people wanted to label it that.' She confessed the routine: she needed sleep so took a pill; needed to stay awake so took something else and combined it with alcohol. The habit crept up insidiously, and it took courage to face the stark reality that she had lost control; it all sounded grotesquely familiar.

Liza has never fully cleared up the

doubts about when or how it all began. Some reports point to the trauma of her mother's death when Liza was twenty-three as the time when she was first prescribed Valium. Others mention a congenital curvature of the spine, which Judy was also said to suffer from; drugs were taken to ease the pain. Then there was her nervous disposition as a child; it is said Valium was given to relieve her anxieties when, according to Liza herself, 'I was so nervous my legs would shake.' Certainly the pressures of making her own way in probably the toughest profession there is, two failed marriages and a third virtually on the rocks, and the tragedy of her miscarriages must all have contributed to her dependency.

But, helped by friends and family, she was to prove that she is one of life's great survivors. She and Mark Gero, himself struggling against similar dependency problems, had separated just before Liza checked into the clinic, but he made regular visits there, reportedly joining in group counselling; and for a while they were to renew their life together — after she checked out of the clinic. At first she seemed reluctant to talk about her experience, but gradually, prompted by probing reporters, she seemed happier to reveal something of her feelings from this time.

She said she didn't mind talking about it because the treatment saved her life. 'Addiction's an incredibly common thing, you know. It's completely understandable. It's very human. And although it's a terrible thing, you don't have to die from it, you can have it fixed,' she confessed to writer Colin Dunne. A life in show business can take its toll, but in the same interview she was adamant that she has never once regretted her life as an entertainer. 'Music keeps my imagination going and it keeps my dreams alive,' she said. 'When it's going well, it's just the best thing in the world, and even the bad bits are . . . well interesting. In this business at least you don't get bored.'

Liza also paid tribute to the help and friendship of Lorna Luft. Lorna, although those few years younger than Liza, had been successfully through the drug problem earlier than her half-sister, and was close by to be a steadying and comforting influence as Liza battled with her problem. Since Lorna had also gone into show business, it was probably inevitable that through the years there would emerge reports of a sisterly rivalry which affected their personal relationships. But Liza insisted that they were always close. What wasn't common knowledge was that after Judy died leaving no provision for her family, Liza supported her half-sister through acting school. There has always been a great deal of affection between them, which extended to Lorna's son Jesse, particularly during his early infant years. Liza told reporter Sue Russell: 'Lorna says that I'm Jesse's second mother. She's my best friend, my sister. She makes me laugh more than anybody, she's got a most ridiculous sense of humour, funny and cutting. She's a marvellous actress and terrific singer — and she's a great mother. My nephew is one of the most divine children I've met.'

Lorna has since proved her talents as a singer and while she has never enjoyed the spectacular, dazzling reputation of Liza, she has shown herself to be a highly professional performer who has established a solid reputation within the shadow of her more celebrated half-sister. In fact as recently as 1992, at the special tribute concert to Sammy Davis Jnr at the Royal Albert Hall in London, *The Times* was moved to comment: ' . . . Judy Garland's girls have done well in showbusiness, but Lorna has always been in big sister Liza's shadow. Until Tuesday night, that is.' Under the headline, *Slinky sis steals the show*, the report went on: ' . . . Lorna, looking sultry in a slinky silver tassled gown and matching high heels . . . sang two numbers that took the roof off — 'Man with a Bugle' and 'I Gotta Be Me'. Here was a salutary lesson in how less can be more from one sibling to another.' Liza would have been delighted to read it.

It didn't take long for Liza to benefit from the process of detoxification of mind and body and she was out of the clinic in less than two weeks, though she continued with a strict therapeutic programme of rehabilitation which lasted several months. Generally reserved about this, Liza has only said that it was intense, revealing and private. It was perhaps here, for the first time, that she fully accepted her mother's death. She told Canada's *Network* magazine: 'I had never had the time, or taken the time, to mourn her or really bury her, the sort of burial that doesn't take place in the ground, but rather in the spirit.'

After leaving the clinic she rested at Liz Taylor's Bel Air mansion and led a quieter life with Mark in their New York home. He had left show business some time earlier to become a sculptor, but their life together was destined to founder. For some time Liza set work and ambition aside. She took time off and seemed to have acquired the ability to relax, to take one day at a time. She rested and slept more. Instead of fighting to live up to the legend of Mama, or pretending she was one of the swinging in-crowd, she accepted that people must see her as Liza Minnelli, an individual, a person and a performer in her own right. As she put it: 'How am I ever going to live up to everything everybody's expecting?' She told *Network*: 'There is this curiosity about me, about my personal life and my career. I guess a large part of it is to see how my life parallels my mother's. I know the curiosity will always be there, so what I do now is to remind myself that this is my life, and I'm going to live it as best I know how.'

It was a revealing statement which showed the extent of her change of attitude, how much more able she was to control her own destiny by simply being herself. 'Being in control of your life is a wonderful thing,' she said. Without forfeiting her drive and ambition she became a more balanced individual, later citing the philosophy that 'you can't change anything but yourself . . . the only thing that can hurt me is me.'

Her fortieth birthday was celebrated on 12 March 1986, a couple of years after her clinical treatment. She said that turning forty was the chance to start all over again with a new and different attitude. 'I felt super,' she added, celebrating with close friends at a private party in London, 'younger than I did at thirty.' One sadness, though, was the death of her father on 25 July that year, aged seventy-six. On television she would narrate a moving tribute to his memory and in her future concerts would remind audiences of the good times they shared and his inspirational influence. Another television date was at the White House on a special programme, *Tribute to American Music*, in which she sang 'Ten Cents a Dance'.

Though her life was more composed and focused, her career still lacked the further dimension of another outright film success. Her ambition to be recognized as a top movie star was still very much alive. There had been nothing to speak of since *Arthur* in 1981, but even then she was only on the periphery of the movie's unexpected triumph, not the major player. *The King of Comedy* back in 1982, the intriguing story of a talk-show host who is kidnapped, was an amusing farce with deeper, even sinister undertones and, although it was rated highly, it was never calculated to advance Liza's career. *The Muppets Take Manhattan* (1984), while probably being the best of the Muppet features, had hardly maintained her movie status even at its then pedestrian level. The best she was able to do the following year was to be included in a line-up of narrators, along with Gene Kelly, Sammy Davis Jnr, Mikhail Baryshnikov and Ray Bolger, for *That's Dancin'*, a movie musical compilation featuring stars like Fred Astaire, Gene Kelly and Eleanor Powell. Hardly surprisingly, the picture made little impact at the box-office.

It wasn't until 1988, seven years after her last mainstream feature, *Arthur*, that Liza Minnelli was back with a significant, if hardly successful, film called *Rent-A-Cop*. It brought the hunky Burt Reynolds once more alongside Liza in an action-packed, suspenseful story which is more essentially about relationships. Liza plays Della Roberts, a lovable former hooker being stalked by a maniacal killer. Tony Church, played by Reynolds, is a hard-nosed ex-cop who has been drummed out of the force, but reluctantly he comes to Della's aid and together they go off to track down the killer.

Liza and Burt had been close friends for some time and she was his first choice for the part, though it nearly didn't happen. Liza had been busy with concerts, but Reynolds was able to use the strength of their relationship, and what he considered a good script, to persuade her to abandon a restful and well earned vacation for filming in Rome. Liza said she was attracted to the role by the sexiness and eccentricity of the character. Typically for Liza, it's an off-beat role, the kind which always seems to capture her interest. She said at the time: 'I'm attracted to characters who are multi-faceted, not just on one level. I like characters who are complicated. They're always more interesting, with lots of dramatic potential.'

The script gave Liza the opportunity to excel as a dramatic actress with a flair for comedy but, although one critic said that she fuelled Della with all the raw sensuality and charisma of a latter day Sally Bowles, the film never looked like becoming a Minnelli tour-de-force in the style of *Cabaret* or even *New York, New York*.

More promising was *Arthur 2: On the Rocks*, filmed on Liza's doorstep in New York, which was released in September

1988. In this sequel to the original smash hit, Arthur Bach, the world's richest and most endearing drunk, is living in grand style with former waitress Linda Marolla as his wife, while the acid-tongued butler Hobson (Sir John Gielgud), who died in the original movie, is resurrected as a phantom at a particularly helpful moment when Arthur has hit rock-bottom again.

Nobody expected there to be another *Arthur* after its director and creator, Steve Gordon, died, but Moore was impressed when a young writer named Andy Breckman came up with a story treatment. Said Dudley: 'He so completely captured the irreverent wit, spirit and joy of the original that I said yes immediately. Then Liza and John Gielgud agreed and, before we knew it, we were in production.'

Liza said she was delighted for the opportunity to play the brassy Linda again. 'Interacting with Dudley is great fun and we both know the characters so well that we can slip into them at a moment's notice,' she added. Dud seemed equally enthusiastic: 'Arthur still lives in a cocoon of wealth and fantasy, but because of the adverse circumstances he encounters, he suddenly has to grow and take on a lot more responsibility for his life. It's that quality of growth in Arthur that attracted me to doing the film,' he said.

This *Arthur* sequel had much to live up to, and by definition was hardly likely to match the original at the box office — which was a pity, considering the positive elements that inspired its creation. Liza said that there had to be something new to say or none of them would have wanted to do a sequel. Maybe it was unfair to compare the two. Producer Robert Shapiro said that the objective was to make a funny movie which would not only appeal to original *Arthur* fans, but also be enjoyed by those who hadn't seen the earlier film. The follow-up was a logical development of the original, but although Shapiro would rate *Arthur 2: On the Rocks* as a picture to make you laugh and also touch your heart, many of the critics found it did neither convincingly.

And the disappointment remained for anyone hoping for a stronger movie profile for Liza, who was still left searching for a screen role good enough to showcase her dramatic, comedic and musical talents. This nonsensical situation continued, a cruel example of the injustice which often vilifies the entertainment business, for her concerts were sell-out successes all over the world, proving her astounding popularity far beyond America.

At the time *Arthur 2* was in production, Liza was feeling a good deal better, both physically and psychologically. She reckoned she had shed ten years since she made the first *Arthur* and was certainly thinner, brighter, more in control; and far less jaded — which was fortunate as the script would confront her with a couple of situations sufficiently real to stir agonizing memories. First was Arthur himself, her screen husband, who is still heavily into drink even if, with her help, he is less of a drunk than in the first story. Giving her greater anguish perhaps was the fact that she and Arthur find they are unable to have a baby and try to adopt. 'I thought I'd never be making a comedy about alcoholism and infertility . . . two things that have occurred in my life,' she said at the time. But it appears that Sir John Gielgud's great experience of life and acting kept her from thinking too much about herself. Liza added: 'You could get into all sorts of psychological depths, but I was sort of inspired by Sir John. Whenever he would hear any kind of deep theory about the stage, his response was always, "Dear girl, it's acting".'

In all, *Arthur 2* must have been a disappointment for Liza in terms of developing her movie career. She had made her first movie more than twenty years before and now, at forty-two years of age, she could still look back to only one comprehensively successful movie. It wasn't that her performances had been inadequate. Even her harshest critics would concede that she had made the best of some pretty shoddy material.

Even her monumental triumph with her one-woman show at Carnegie Hall in 1987 seemed to have had little impression on the movie makers. It was a consummate performance and her three-week continuous engagement, incorporating sixteen appearances between May 28 and June 18, set an outright record for the hall in the whole of its illustrious 96-year history.

Publicized by a 43 ft high poster which would dominate Times Square, and backed for the first time by a 46-piece orchestra which included 24 string instruments — somewhat different from her normal 12-piece backing group — it was the engagement of a lifetime, and enabled her to include much new material along with her, by now, obligatory standards such as 'Cabaret', 'Maybe This Time' and, of course, 'New York, New York'. Liza's regular drummer and musical director, Bill La Vorgna, who had been Liza's musical mentor and 'father figure' for the past ten years — she had known him since she was a child and he worked with Judy — was with her for this special occasion, as were lyricist Fred Ebb and composer Marvin Hamlisch.

Ebb had shadowed almost every step of Liza's developing career since he picked her out as a special kind of talent during the run of *Best Foot*

Forward more than twenty years before, subsequently writing almost all of her most successful material. Over the years there has developed between them a special kind of relationship. Liza often talks about him as her 'best, best friend' — a kind of big brother to her. She obviously has a great deal of respect and admiration for Ebb, explaining at the time of the concert that he combined a great sense of the theatrical with down-to-earth common sense. Their closeness at both personal and professional levels has been a major factor in her development as a concert performer. Liza explains it like this: 'Together we've figured out a form of variety performance that is more than a nightclub act. And I think the reason I've never faltered on that road is because I've always had Fred's good taste behind me. He's a wonderful director, but he's also nice.'

Ebb wrote and directed this latest Carnegie Hall show which, in addition to having Bill La Vorgna as musical director, was costumed by Liza's long-time friend and fashion designer Halston, and had musical arrangements by Marvin

Hamlisch who had devotedly continued to be her friend and sometime arranger since their schooldays together at Scarsdale High.

The occasion itself yielded more perhaps than even Liza could have expected. Reviews were jubilant. Clarke Taylor's report in the *Los Angeles Times* began: 'The most electrifying opening night of the musical season here took place not on Broadway but at Carnegie Hall where Liza Minnelli opened a three-week engagement. The glittery event, attended by a Who's Who of the Broadway musical theater, brightened up a lackluster season and once again lit up Minnelli's career.'

The programme was a cavalcade of songs from her 23-year career in show business, but she had worked well with her collaborators to make it much more than that. It was reflective of her life, her current outlook. She mentioned her late father and mother; and she alluded to her recent personal problems by altering the lyrics of 'Cabaret'. Instead of 'I made my mind up back in Chelsea, when I go I'm going like Elsie' (a woman who has died 'happy' from too much pills and liquor), she re-worded the ending: ' . . . I'm NOT going like Elsie.' The report noted it as one of the most pointed and poignant references of the evening.

Even the irritatingly fickle acoustics and amplification system withered against the spectacular triumph of the evening. The *Hollywood Reporter* told its readers: 'The millions of dollars spent on renovating Carnegie Hall were almost nullified when Liza Minnelli appeared on stage before a 46-piece orchestra and practically demolished the rafters, the balconies, the ushers, the paying customers and anything/anyone else within earshot of her voice. Her stunning performance alone could have done it, but the glittering crowd (ranging from Dolly Parton to Helen Hayes, Walter Cronkite to Bob Fosse, Alan King to Kevin Bacon) would certainly have been held partially responsible since it began raising the roof at 8.08 p.m. and didn't stop until the last note of the last song.' There to applaud her triumph, in addition to Lorna Luft, were former husbands Peter Allen and Jack Haley Jnr, and her husband for the past seven years, Mark Gero.

The programme was a singing, swinging mixture of old and new, and included most if not all the material particularly associated with Liza. For this special occasion Liza had dispensed with background singers, there were no high-kicking dancers and nobody telling jokes to set up her entry. 'How High the Moon' was performed unusually and effectively with a single violin accompaniment. A Kander and Ebb medley included established favourites and little-known melodies. With all those strings Liza was able to sing songs like Harold Arlen's 'I Never Have Seen Snow'. 'I've always wanted to sing that particular song,' she announced. And there were popular standards like 'How Deep is the Ocean' and, perhaps most moving of all, an interlude of 'songs my daddy taught me'. Reported *Variety* on this major Carnegie Hall triumph: 'She sang through some special material, never overdoing, always maintaining a classy sense of balance and, maybe most important, always in total control.' Afterwards, at a party to celebrate the show, a particularly upbeat Liza would declare: 'Work agrees with me!'. Her critically acclaimed performance was dutifully recorded and made available internationally in September 1987. The digitally recorded double album *Liza Minnelli 'Live' at Carnegie Hall* promptly became a best-seller and one of the music industry's most highly praised live concert recordings.

It was appropriate that this huge success for Liza would have as its background New York City, because nothing epitomizes the spectacle, style, charisma and excitement of the performer as this most special, for her, of cities. Only a short time before, her version of 'New York, New York' had been designated New York City's official song by Mayor Koch. Responded Liza: 'It is such a thrill to know that a song written for me about my favourite city in the world has become Manhattan's theme song. New York, New York . . . it is the greatest city in the world and, to quote the song, it really is true that "if I can make it there, I'd make it anywhere".'

Except Hollywood perhaps . . .

But elsewhere Liza Minnelli's success

continued unabated. Later in 1987 she completed a highly successful tour of Europe with Michael Feinstein. The schedule was punishing. The tour opened in Genoa on 2 October and took seven weeks, the last date being played at the Lido in Paris. The programme took in seven countries with a schedule of city dates which included Florence, Rome, Naples, Milan, Munich, Vienna, Stuttgart, Frankfurt, Berlin, Hamburg, Dusseldorf, Brussels and London. The show was a nucleus of the Carnegie Hall presentation, adapted for the road. Feinstein would later pay Liza the compliment of labelling her perhaps the greatest entertainer of our time. 'I mean, who's like her?' he went on. 'Barbra Streisand has a great voice, but she can't do what Liza can do. How many total entertainers are left? We used to have a lot of them, but how many do we have now who can sing and dance and can be dramatic and funny? Liza has everything.'

Among her dates in 1988 was a 'good old-fashioned programme of song and dance', when Liza teamed with Ben

Vereen in a charity concert which mixed swinging numbers like 'Alexander's Ragtime Band' with tender ballads and a lively mixture which inevitably included 'Cabaret' and 'Liza With a Z'. 'New York, New York' was the scheduled encore.

The hectic pace continued through 1988. She worked on a TV special with Fred Ebb, completed filming the second *Arthur* movie, and among an almost continuing run of personal appearances, Liza played to packed houses at the Trump Plaza in Atlantic City in May. All five concerts were sold out. A remarkable coincidence brought Lorna Luft to Atlantic City at the same time, so both sisters managed to see each other's show and catch up on all the latest gossip. After an absence of seven years, Liza returned to the Las Vegas nightclub stage in November that year with performances at the Riviera Hotel and Casino and was in such outstanding form that Don Usherson of the *Las Vegas Review Journal* wrote: 'I have seen more than 600 stage performances in the seven years that she has been gone. I have never seen a greater one than I saw this night. Eight times the Riviera audience interrupted her songs with thunderous applause and cheering. Like the greatest — Al Jolson, Sammy Davis Jnr, Charles Aznavour — every song is a performance. A marvellously exhilarating theatrical experience.'

And 1988 was also the vintage year that Liza teamed with Sinatra and Sammy in their triumvirate, *The Ultimate Event*. This ambitious celebration, described by one writer as 'an unabashed valentine' to the three of them, had emerged from an idea of Sinatra's in the autumn of 1987 that he, Sammy and Dean Martin, from their 1960s 'Rat Pack' days, should embark on an extensive tour visiting US cities they wouldn't normally visit. Thus in early March 1987, *Frank, Dean and Sammy Together Again* opened in Oakland, California to packed houses. In fact the 'old timers' reunion' had such an impact that the first three months of the tour were sold out in advance of that very first performance in Oakland.

Dean Martin, less enthusiastic initially than the others because of personal problems and his physically frail condition, found the rigours of travel and playing to such large audiences too exhausting and soon had to withdraw. For the time being Frank and Sammy continued on their own, the show being cleverly renamed *Frank and Sammy — Two for the Road.* But long before the new autumn series was due to begin, the sponsors American Express, tour manager Elliot Kasmer, Frank and Sammy had agreed that a replacement for Dean was necessary.

By the time the show arrived in New York both Frank and Sammy had made up their minds. Said Liza: 'First Sammy called to ask me if I would like to appear in the autumn series. Two days later Frank called and asked me the same question.'

At first Liza found the prospect of appearing with two performers of such legendary stature intimidating, if not frightening, in spite of her own considerable experience; but it was the opportunity of a lifetime. Repackaged and under a new, if somewhat cumbersome title — *Frank, Liza and Sammy, The Ultimate Event* — the new series went on tour in October 1988 and played to packed houses all over the United States.

Said music critic Boni Anthony Johnson: 'Not since the halcyon days of the great package tours have we seen a triple bill as loaded with talent.' There would be Sammy performing with the energy of a man half his sixty-two years, joking and of course singing with that beautifully rounded and melodious voice. 'What Kind of Fool am I' had to be included. Next out would be Liza, going through her well-known show tunes, vamping with a man's hat as she brought back vivid memories of *Cabaret*. Sinatra came last, in his mid-seventies still a giant of an entertainer, with such songs as 'Where or When' and 'For Once in My Life'. The finale would see all three on stage, clowning and, above all, singing their hearts out.

The tour would take in more than twenty engagements in eleven cities, but as the schedule was not concentrated, there was time for Liza to fit in other commitments, like TV commercials and personal appearances. The stars of *The Ultimate Event* soon acquired the tagline of The Ultimate Trio. An impressed and excited Minnelli commented: 'You're looking at sixty years of music here.' Liza also enjoyed the companionship of sharing the floor with two other performers. She had told *Celebrity Spotlight* earlier that year: 'I think the main reason that I want to do more film is because of the collaboration, because of the people. You're so alone when you're out there doing concerts.' And about those films she had obviously become more philosophical. 'You've got to always go with what you feel you can relate to. Sometimes you just have to wait for something you can believe in.'

The Ultimate Event never lost its sparkle and made a major impact with tours of Australia and Europe. But after Sammy's tragic illness and death, Liza would lament that it never seemed quite the same, though Liza and Frank were to continue for some time. But despite being arguably the world's foremost female live entertainer, Hollywood still wasn't falling over itself with good movie contracts. Could her enormous impact as a live performer in some way be the real reason? For, despite her renewed assertions in a number of recent interviews that she wanted to do more filming, nothing seemed to give her quite the buzz of a live performance going really well. Three years later, when talking to Lesley White of *The Sunday Times*, she put it as simply as this: 'I guess I just got stuck with Broadway because it was what I knew, I understood the lyrics and it was a novelty to have someone my age doing it.' White further interpreted the enigma: 'Songs are how she understands the world. For her stage shows she treats every evening as if it were a little movie, even keeping notes on all the characters she imagines to be in the songs, what colour hair they have, how they wear their clothes. Singing, she insists, comes from acting.' And Liza herself added: 'And the best performances come from truth . . . Sammy taught me that.'

At the time of her Carnegie Hall concert she revealed with obvious enthusiasm: 'The moments that are the best on stage are when you're really in tune with the audience, and you almost feel like it's a conversation between two people. That's when the magic happens.'

There have been some notable examples of success in both movies and concerts/cabaret — Frank Sinatra is the supreme case — but perhaps the problem arises when you try to run the two careers concurrently. Sinatra's main concert performances came at the end of his film career. And maybe it is harder for a woman. Streisand did both for a short time, but even she might have run into problems had she not voluntarily relinquished her career as a live entertainer. And she, too, complained about the shortage of good parts for women and was forced into organizing and managing her own movie projects to satisfy her creative talent.

The small screen however has proved itself somewhat keener to utilise Liza's dramatic talent. She played her first dramatic role on television as the heroically simple Mary Lou Weisman, a mother coping with her son's muscular dystrophy, in *A Time to Live*, which received a Golden Globe award in 1985, and followed this with *Liza Minnelli: Triple*

Play. The novelty of this project was that she played three different characters in three separate story lines. In the first segment she is a Coney Island hooker opposite Ryan O'Neal's pimp in a dramatic tale. The second segment is a comedy with Liza playing a dreams-thwarted New York hoofer who meets a magical African king. Fred Ebb and John Kander wrote the third, a mini-musical set in the 1950s. In these music, comedy and drama playlets Liza more than adequately proved her versatility. Ebb touched a truism when he commented: 'She's a girl who has had disappointments in her life. So she's best in songs that are actable, stories which are filled with a wide range of meaningful emotion.'

There is little to argue about that and, taking the example of *Cabaret* particularly, along with her prodigious reputation as an entertainer, you would think it would not have been beyond the wit of Hollywood, for selfish reasons if nothing else, to generate a suitable motion picture for Liza Minnelli. Given her reputation and the right vehicle, she could have made a fortune for them as she had done with *Cabaret*.

But it would be 1991 before her next film would be released. Before then she would raise the proverbial eyebrows again and move in an altogether surprising direction. But as Liza has always maintained: you have to follow your heart in this business.

10

New Songs for Old

LIZA MINNELLI astonished even her most liberal of fans when she made a strong sortie into the world of pop and rock in the late 1980s. She dropped the hint in 1988 when she took the unprecedented step of working on a rock'n'roll record, with Gene Simmons, the outrageous bass player from Kiss, acting as producer. Nor should it be forgotten that she had worked with Alice Cooper as long ago as 1973 when, according to one authority, the original shock-rocker was at the zenith of his fame.

But it wasn't a totally alarming time for the traditional Minnelli follower. She continued to do plenty of personal appearances, made her debut in a television commercial in 1988 singing a snatch of the Kander-Ebb song 'City Lights' for which it is estimated she received more than $1 million, and in January 1989 she was presented in concert at The McCallum Theatre, Palm Desert, California, by the Betty Ford Center with the Eisenhower Hospital Concert.

In her first television commercial Liza was seen in four well-known New York locations. She was dancing outside the Plaza Hotel, at the Joyce Theatre, the Empire Diner and at the Fulton Ferry landing. She was backed by the Carnegie Hall concert orchestra; and husband Mark Gero had a cameo role. The lyrics of 'City Lights' were of course changed for the commercial, which was to promote a new fragrance for men called 'Metropolis' from Estée Lauder. The fifteen-month contract included a number of personal appearances in the cosmetics departments of major stores.

Liza explained at the time that she had known Mrs Lauder for more than twenty years, having first met at a party in the south of France. After that Mrs Lauder became almost like a member of the family. 'She's what America means to me in a certain way,' said Liza. 'In a sea of men there's this terrific lady who started in her kitchen and grabbed life by the shoulders and marched right on.' It appears that when Estée Lauder personally called Liza she said she wanted to portray the energy and life of New York City in her TV commercial and wanted Liza to help her. Liza quickly agreed.

A very different assignment was her concert for the Betty Ford Center and the Eisenhower Hospital. Betty Ford said: 'When Liza Minnelli offers to sing for you and for a cause close to your heart, such as the Betty Ford Center, you say yes immediately and with great enthusiasm.'

Liza dutifully and tunefully recorded the help the clinic had been to her personally by opening her programme of seventeen songs with, significantly, 'I Can See Clearly Now'. *The Desert Sun* reported: 'Some members of the audience, including such dapper-looking stars as Betty and Gerald Ford, Gregory Peck, Sammy Davis Jnr, Dolores Hope and Barbara Sinatra, said they could see the effect of her rejuvenation. She was vibrant, oozing with personality and sounding as sensitive and robust as one might expect from a Tony, Oscar, Golden Globe and Emmy Award-winning performer in her prime.'

It was also an expensive, elegant occasion. With tickets priced at $1,500 each, it was fitting that the evening should begin with a formal dinner at the nearby Morningside Club, after which guests travelled to the theatre to be greeted by the up-market presence of a chamber quartet and waiters who proffered champagne and Perrier. As the press report suggested: 'It was a beautiful crowd. Men in tuxedos, women in sequined theatre suits and long gowns — everyone elegant.' Liza's choice to open her performance was a very short, peach-coloured sequined dress and jacket; later she changed it for a sexy blue and black sequined trouser outfit. An occasion of some self-indulgence it may well have been, but so what? The purpose had been achieved, to raise half a million dollars for the Ford Center and the emergency room of the Eisenhower Medical Center.

The show which followed was vintage Liza and showcased her artistry in weaving her material into a cleverly constructed presentation. The opening was strong and attention-grabbing and there was the usual big Broadway-style finish. In between was the easy, confident flow of Minnelli standards, always interesting, frequently amusing and sometimes new and surprising; inevitably, highly professional.

If her support for the Betty Ford Center and the associated Eisenhower Hospital Auxiliary was predictable in terms of an expression of personal gratitude to the former, it was also not unexpected. She has gained an estimable reputation over the years for the unstinting support she has given to a number of organizations as diverse as The International Red Cross, Muscular Dystrophy Association and the American Foundation for AIDS.

Of particular concern is the Philadelphia-based Institutes for the Achievement of Human Potential. She serves as a member of the board of directors. This organization concerns itself with helping children who are severely brain-damaged to attain average levels of function. The programmes are sometimes extremely complex and involve hours of careful therapy, with parents being taught what they can do on a daily basis to contribute to the process of recovery. Liza has given concerts to help provide funds and is known for her generosity in making personal donations for specific requirements. A cheque for $10,000 which chairman Glenn Doman received one day in early 1987 enabled the Institutes to buy ten special respiratory patterning machines which meant they could complete their programme of treatment. Without the money ten children could well have been deprived of the chance of an improved standard of life, possibly of life itself.

But by far the greatest surprise for Minnelli fans in the late 1980s occurred in 1989. For it was during her time in London doing *The Ultimate Event* shows with Frank and Sammy, that Liza was also diving into the recording studio with Britain's pop duo, the Pet Shop Boys. It is probably true to say she had been wanting to make a temporary change of direction for some time because, despite a hit like 'Liza With a Z', she had never seen herself as a successful recording artist. Certainly she had never had a hit in the modern pop chart. When she signed a new contract with CBS and they asked her who she wanted to work with, she mentioned the Pet Shop Boys.

She was forced to explain in order to counter their astonishment and disbelief. 'I heard a song called 'Rent' about a year and a half ago, and I thought "Now who wrote that?" 'Cos the words are wonderful and it's a beautiful melody, and yet it's got a good beat to it, and that's what attracted me to Neil and Chris, the lyrical content of what they write,' she told the *Guardian*.

And in August 1989 her soaring electro-ballet 'Losing My Mind', written specially for her by Neil Tennant and Chris Lowe — the Pet Shop Boys — put her in the pop charts for the first time ever. An excited Liza blurted out: 'It's the first time ever that a song has been written for me . . . and the first time I've had a hit record.'

The success was unexpected, particularly as the song was an up-dated version of the old Stephen Sondheim melody from the show *Follies*. *Results*, the album from which Liza's pop single hit was taken, was released a couple of months later through Epic Records, and was destined to bring her yet another major award. The spectacular sales of this, her first pop album, would be enough to earn her a gold disc. At the time she pronounced it to be the most exciting award she had received: ' . . . because it's my first and it's for something I've never done before.'

But despite this phenomenal success, and the subsequent impact on the charts of 'Love Pains', one of her other Pet Shop Boys' singles, her traditional following had no cause to fear this was the end of an era. Liza's penchant was still for musical standards dating back almost to her mother's era. Nor, she pointed out, was this the thin edge of the wedge: there were no plans to update other material, she assured them.

There is no doubt that in moving away from 'traditional Minnelli' she had taken quite a gamble. She elaborated, putting the risk into context: 'It's real safe when you're successful doing one thing and it's real tempting to stay there. But then you get to a point in your own life, in your own self (Liza was forty-three at the time) when it's okay to risk,' she told the *Guardian*. 'It's okay if people don't like it. When they do like it, it's just phenomenal, and that's what's happening to me right now.'

But maybe having been an entertainer for more than twenty-five years, Liza was merely showing just what a clever old showbiz veteran she was, for the Pet Shop Boys were not new to remodelling jobs. Two years before they had given Dusty Springfield's career a boost, sending her soaring up to No 1 in the charts after she didn't even have a record contract. But while never suggesting that this change of direction was to be permanent — it would be hard to visualize the full-voiced, theatrical Liza permanently ensconced in the sanitized rock and pop culture of the Pet Shop Boys — she was at pains to point out that neither was this collaboration a cheap gimmick to put her into the musical headlines. And she certainly didn't need the cash! She saw it more as an extension of what she had

Her powerful performance in *The Sterile Cuckoo* (*Pookie* in the UK) in 1969 secured an Oscar nomination.

Wearing her hair long for *Charlie Bubbles*. The eyes belong to Vincente, but it's no surprise she's Judy's daughter.

With her greatest
friend, her mother.

Liza with her
mother and director
George Abbott.

Seen with co-star Ken Howard in *Tell Me That You Love Me, Junie Moon*. Liza's 'scarred face' can be clearly seen in this still from the movie.

The film version of *Cabaret* brought international cinema stardom. With Joel Grey at the Kit Kat Klub.

In a quieter personal moment with co-star Michael York (Brian Roberts) enjoying life in pre-war Berlin.

With Robert De Niro in *New York, New York* (1977), Liza was in her element singing musical standards as well as the title song, which became her theme tune.

been doing, citing the case that she had sung the tuneful melodies of many of the songwriters who were now dead, adding: 'I now want to sing Neil and Chris's songs. They are some of the best new writers around.'

And she put forward another angle which many of her admirers might have largely overlooked. 'Although I had been singing pop music on stage for years, I'd never recorded it. It was Gene Simmons of Kiss who persuaded me to take the plunge,' she explained. What she felt was so right about the project was that she didn't have to make compromises. She apparently went into the studio like the proverbial bull, all set to cast off her long traditions and come on like your regular rock star. But Neil soon put her right, she explained.

The album *Results* would include seven of the Pet Shop Boys' songs, but if Liza secretly hoped that the success of 'Losing My Mind' would edge her towards mainstream pop and a permanent younger audience, then both she and they would be disappointed. For despite the enormous and unexpected success, nothing further happened to make this one-off collaboration more than just that. While it lasted, however, Liza threw herself into the project with typical energy, style and panache. She recalled that they had first met at London's Mayfair Hotel, where she had been staying, and immediately got on well. As a preliminary she had met the boys at a studio in New York when they tried out 'Tonight is Forever'. The recording session was fun by all accounts and she said that she never imagined that they would end up laughing so much.

The combination of Liza and the Pet Shop Boys was a difficult concept for her friends in America to accept. They at first thought that she meant that she had agreed to do some backing vocals as a favour to the Pet Shop Boys, or they thought they might just be doing a single together. Given her depth of show business experience and an impressive array of the topmost honours in almost every branch of entertainment, it's easy to imagine their stunned silence when she explained that they had consented to produce her album. Even more astounding was her admission: 'I trusted them so much that I didn't have to ask any questions about the sort of LP it would be. I just said "I'll do whatever you want because this is new to me — you're the boss".' Even Liza, on reflection, found it amazing that, after thirty years in the business, she could place so much trust in them.

Not surprisingly, Liza took the opportunity to have fun. She and the boys were reported to be almost inseparable as they took her round London town to dine at all the smart places and occasionally venturing to some of the more notorious raves. Rumoured one daily tabloid: 'Neil Tennant, thirty-five, even gave in to her pleading and delayed the start of his summer holiday so that they could go together to see *Batman*.'

When one journalist brought up the subject of the popularity of the Pet Shop Boys around the gay club circuit and their reputed camp connection, suggesting that it came partly because they were happy to burlesque the genre, Liza's reported response was an astonished: 'God, I never thought of that.' She sensibly refused to be drawn, saying it was none of her business, that she was close to both of them and they had never been offensive or overtly strange to her. It was vintage Minnelli, however, when they appeared on *Wogan*, gushing and extrovert, she clapped her arms around a shocked and embarrassed Chris and kissed him. And as the *Mirror* gleefully reported: 'She made straight-faced Neil Tennant laugh out loud and smile for the cameras and only just failed in her attempts to get them both to go with her to a lunch with Princess Diana. They obviously fell for the Minnelli magic. Tennant enthused: 'Liza is fabulous, but the thing about Liza is that she is fabulous all the time.' Who could have asked for more?

Her exploration into the pop field, despite its remarkable success, would continue to excite speculation and while some would suggest that the whole thing was high camp, a gigantic send up, which she would emphatically deny ('no we didn't want to do anything like that'), there were many others who found it hard to appreciate the schizophrenic nature of her musical world. She explained: 'People are always fascinated by Neil going to dinner with me and Frank Sinatra as if they're from two different worlds. They got on fine.'

Now, more than four years later, the association of Liza Minnelli and the Pet Shop Boys, who at that time had eighteen consecutive British top 20 hit singles, retains enigmatic overtones. In trying to explain her feelings she has said that she was always impressed by Neil's lyrics. 'He writes almost like what I call pop poetry,' she once said. 'Even with a driving beat and an intent that's out-and-out rock'n'roll he's saying something too on top of it, which does make a difference to me, that the words are often important.' One of the more astonishing images from those days, which even now is likely to prompt Liza to raise an eyebrow and widen her smile, is her successful appearance for the first time on television's *Top of the Pops* at the ripe old age of forty-three. At the time it all brought her back into media attention with a vengeance.

11

Liza in London Town

WHEN Liza Minnelli was in London in 1974 she realized she was a star. They measured her for a wax model of herself for Madame Tussauds. London has moved significantly in and out of Liza's life for business and pleasure almost since she was a baby. Years before when Judy was waging war with Sid Luft and there were fearful wrangles over the custody of the three children, Judy had gathered her brood together and swept them off to London with her where she was booked to do a number of stage performances.

Judy loved the place and Liza had no choice as a child other than to travel with her. When later the choice was hers alone she still kept coming back. If not quite her second home, the British capital certainly appears to occupy a special place in her affections. At the time of her whirlwind romance with Peter Sellers she had every intention of buying or renting a house or apartment in London. She has achieved great success in London and is not slow to take every opportunity to return to the scene of some of her major triumphs.

Pragmatic in many spheres of her life, Liza also has a sense of history and sensitivity to what has gone on before. In those early days with her mother they would stay at the Savoy. Whenever she is in town, Liza is still inclined to head for the Strand and the world-famous Thames-side hotel which retains star status from earlier times. In 1989 she was interviewed there by both the *Guardian* and the *TV Times*. Two years later, when the *Daily Mirror* wanted to interview her, she invited them to the Savoy. A year earlier she had ordered scrambled eggs and iced tea in the Savoy restaurant when interviewed by the *Tatler*; then couldn't resist the waiter's invitation and added bacon and tomatoes. And it was in another interview at the Savoy with Frank Bough, when London was chosen to hold the Royal

World Charity Premiere of *Stepping Out*, that she revealed that she comes back to England at least three times a year. She couldn't remember just how many times she had visited the place.

Liza as a youngster lived for a short time in London. Her best friend then was Katie Manning, with whom she is said still to keep in touch. She completed some of her education in London, achieving the British equivalent of the American high school diploma. When she was sixteen Liza returned to London to live with her mother and the rest of the family when Judy was shooting *I Could Go on Singing*, which turned out to be her last picture. Dirk Bogarde and Jack Klugman starred in this specially-tailored screenplay about an American singing star in Britain trying to take over her illegitimate son from her one-time lover, but who eventually finds the pull of the footlights stronger.

It is always a major media event when Liza comes to town. The transatlantic links were reinforced when she wanted to expand her musical horizons. For her successful incursion into the pop medium she chose not only to link up with an outstandingly successful British duo, but continued the connection with London by recording in the studios of the West-End-based Epic Records. She was appearing with Frank Sinatra and Sammy Davis Jnr at the Albert Hall at the time and told Michael Aspel and William Shatner on British television that life in London on this visit was particularly hectic. 'I'd be at the Albert Hall, very posh and wonderful, and would then tear across town and into the studios at night after the show. I'd bring back the tapes so that Frank and Sammy could listen to them the following day.'

Though Liza married for the first time at a ceremony in New York, it was in London that she first met singer, pianist and composer/arranger Peter Allen, along with his partner Chris Bell, on their arrival from their homeland of Australia. Some years later she taped a TV special in London with Charles Aznavour, an almost lifelong friend.

Liza has become a legendary 'live' performer in London and over more than a decade has been able to 'sell out' her dates and engagements in the capital. She has happy memories of her mother's outstanding concert successes in London and the historic Palladium became almost as familiar to her as Carnegie Hall or the Winter Garden in New York. Her links go back more than forty years, to 1951 when, as a 5-year-old, she saw her mother's debut at the Palladium. Fifteen years later she was the star attraction herself at London's popular nightspot, the Talk of the Town; seven years on she was presenting her one-woman show at the Palladium. In fact Liza said on one of her visits that her last concert performance with her mother was at the Palladium.

She has made some significant personal and professional comments and decisions during her stays in London. One of the most revealing, and surprising perhaps, was in the late 1980s, again in an interview at the Savoy: 'Every time I've made a move forward in my life or done something brave or new or modern, it's always been in this country,' she said. She felt that musically people in Britain were much more open. 'And I lived a lot of my life here,' she reminded readers, talking from the hotel suite she and her mother always stayed in all those years ago. (She occupies the same rooms whenever she returns.) She told another reporter: 'I would love to work here on the West End stage. But I don't want to do something for the sake of it.' It is surprising that the opportunity has never happened. Talking on British television she said: 'Some of the best times I ever had have been in this country.'

The attraction of London for Liza is not hard to define. Despite her Hollywood ambitions she has always been in love with the essential elements of traditional big-city life, the pace, excitement, the strong and concentrated focus, the tensions, noise, bustle; and the size and instant impact of it all. New York captured her imagination and her heart long ago. London comes close to it and as a bonus bears the singular distinction of being a bold and arrogant capital city. And often when she comes visiting there seems to be yet one more 'royal' to meet. She appeared in her first Royal Command Performance at the Palladium in 1972.

Often her visits to the UK are part of a wider European tour, as in 1990 when she came to London to promote her latest single 'Love Pains'. In February she had been in Germany to receive the Golden Camera award for her 'outstanding success and new style of music'. Michael Douglas and Ben Kingsley received Golden Cameras in Germany at the same time as Liza. It was while she was back in London again that she revealed for the first time the details of her visit to East Berlin where she was astonished to be recognized by youngsters who seemed to know all about her and her music.

She had arrived in London around the middle of the month and immediately was recruited as an 'award presenter' rather than receiver at the annual BAFTA awards, announcing Fine Young Cannibals as the winner of the best album by a British artist. Two days later she was at the BBC studios to record 'Love Pains' for the television chart show *Top of the Pops*, but after entering the charts at an optimistic number 50, it only moved up nine places before fading away. Her first British broadcast of the new single was on the Saturday morning television youth show *Going Live* where she was also interviewed by the two presenters and members of the audience, some in the studio and others through a phone link to listeners. Answering a variety of questions she told her young audience . . . yes, when she lived here she lost her American accent — slightly; that of all the awards she had won the one she treasured most was the gold record for *Results* (really?). She responded to 'Jenny's' question about a remaining ambition by saying, after a little thought, 'I'd like to play in a club where you could come to see me' — thereby making a young girl's day; and she revealed her most embarrassing moment: she was at a fancy club, with a lot of snooty people, and had to introduce Florence Henderson. Not knowing who she was, she asked a waiter who told her she was an ice skater. So she gave Florence the big build up, only to discover that she was not an ice skater at all, but a very fine opera singer.

It was that same evening that she

was joined by *Star Trek*'s Captain Kirk (William Shatner) on the popular *Aspel & Co*, again singing her new single. Her performance was a revelation. Dressed in black trousers and jacket with her hair soft and short, she started the number quietly and with restraint against a double-rhythm backing — no sense of Liza belting out a song here. Her delivery was more dramatic, though still well controlled, after flinging off her jacket to reveal a strapless top with a neckline which dived down almost to the waist.

She was back in London again in 1991, this time to boost *Stepping Out*. Former Aussie 'soap' star Jason Donovan, at twenty-three, was suitably impressed by the legendary Liza when she took a nostalgic walk backstage at the Palladium, where he was starring in the Andrew Lloyd Webber-Tim Rice musical *Joseph and the Amazing Technicolor Dreamcoat*.

Liza's screen career has threaded its way in and around the old country to a surprising degree for a girl who is so prominently 'all-American'. It was a British picture which gave Liza that hard earned break into the all-important main feature movie scene, even if her role was modest. *Charlie Bubbles* in 1967 was not only a British-made picture, financed by British money, but, Liza aside, it also had a comprehensively British cast. And that initial, priceless experience of working on a filmset for the first time as an adult was obtained in the UK.

Five years later the 1972-released *Cabaret*, while essentially an American product though made in Germany, had the very British Michael York, born in Buckinghamshire, as Liza's co-star lover. And then after ten years when nobody in Hollywood was very much interested in Liza Minnelli, and with her movie career in the doldrums, it was the London-born Lewis Gilbert who negotiated her movie re-birth with *Stepping Out*, which also of course featured Britain's Julie Walters. It was Gilbert who told Liza: 'They'd forgotten how good you are' and then, despite her doubts and nervousness at doing a major musical picture for the first time in fourteen years, made the point that: 'All you needed was someone to believe in you.' Liza continued to

have the highest regard for the British
director. 'Lewis believed in all of us,'
she said. 'It was so wonderful working
with him. We (the troupe) all had to
learn to tap together and we spent three
weeks, eight hours a day, six days a week,
working like slaves . . . but Lewis has a
particular gift for working with women.
It was great fun.'

Even during those miserably barren
movie years between *New York, New
York* in 1977 and *Stepping Out* in
1991, it was mainly Britain which
prevented her slide into film obscurity.
The performances of Sir John Gielgud
(born London) and Dudley Moore
(born Essex) — an Oscar and Oscar
nomination respectively — were crucial
to the success of *Arthur* in 1981.
And it was *Arthur*'s success at the
box office which brought their co-star
back into focus as a movie star. It
was also the film's sequel, *Arthur 2:
On the Rocks* in 1988, again strongly
influenced by the two British actors,
which helped Liza recover from the
seven long and demoralizing years of
The King of Comedy, The Muppets

Take Manhattan, *That's Dancin'* (as narrator) and *Rent-A-Cop*.

And it was in London in 1991 that a revitalized Liza cast aside her recent divorce from Mark Gero with the honest declaration that she was enjoying the greatest time of her life. She left no-one in doubt that she considered the final break from Gero to be a definite success. 'I am proud of the way we have handled it,' she told the *Daily Mirror*. 'We had a good run. We were together for twelve years.'

In London too, during a television interview with Barry Norman on *Film '91*, she articulated her approach to her profession, and in so doing conveyed her sincerity and conviction as an artist. Because of who her mother and father were, did the public expect more from her than from other people?, Norman asked. She considered her words carefully and spoke relatively slowly. 'Well, they expect a lot . . . but . . . er . . . I've led them to believe they can . . . [slight pause] . . . you know you set yourself up for whatever you get; it's your own responsibility what happens to you.'

It was also Norman who, largely ignoring the fact that her stay at the Betty Ford Clinic was a sensitive issue, managed to use the experience to elicit other fundamental features of the Minnelli character and her attitude to her profession and life in general. 'What did all that experience teach you about yourself?' he enquired.

Liza's response: 'The metaphor in the film *Stepping Out*, . . . *we can* do what *I can't* do, is everything I learned; the support of other people; the faith that we can make it work; that one day at a time . . . all of the stuff that you learn about yourself; the fear of yesterday and the, well, let's say the regrets of yesterday and the fear of tomorrow are very heavy things, so that if you can go one day at a time, if you can learn one tap step a day — *just one* — if you can just work with that cane — *just today* — you don't have to worry about tomorrow . . . you know, the hat (moving her hand to adjust an imaginary top hat to the correct position on her head) . . . . *just today* I'm going to learn to do this with the hat. That's how I was kinda thinking when I was doing *Stepping Out*.' It was a revelation when she explained on British television that she suffered from arthritis of the hip and that keeping moving and dancing helped a great deal.

But London has also been the backdrop to some disappointments for her fans, particularly those in the UK. It was in 1991 that Mike Morris of *TV-am* asked her if she had any ambitions as yet unfulfilled. She said that for the last twelve years there was always one role she wanted to do and that was the part of Roxy Hart in the musical *Chicago*. 'And yesterday, Lewis, Lewis Gilbert, announced that we were going to make the film — so that was like a dream come the yesterday for me. Oh, I'm so excited,' revealed Liza. When Morris further asked when it would all happen a less definite Liza added: 'That won't start for at least eight months.' Sadly the film has yet to emerge.

And in 1993 Liza was confidently expected to return to the Royal Albert Hall — probably in November — with her latest presentation. But as early as May the prospect looked doubtful because, it was thought, no suitable venue could be found which would fit in with Liza's available dates.

12

Stepping Out

THOUGH Liza Minnelli is the archetypal American female entertainer, driven by the deep-rooted traditions and instincts of show business, Hollywood for all its expertise and experience had seemed incapable of finding a suitable outlet for her varied talents. Her supporting roles in *Arthur* and *Arthur 2* aside, they hadn't come up with anything that meant very much for over twelve years, when London-born veteran director Lewis Gilbert happened on the scene.

A director of considerable skill and intuition, he had been in the movie business from childhood. He was an actor before the war when he appeared with Laurence Olivier in *The Divorce of Lady X* in 1938, and then, after being invalided out of the RAF in 1944, and on his own admission being too shy to continue acting, he worked as a director with a particular talent for documentaries.

He made his name through war pictures, which drew on his experience of documentary techniques, and in the 1950s produced some epics of the genre with *Albert RN*, *Reach for the Sky* (which was the story of wartime fighter ace Douglas Bader), and *Carve Her Name with Pride* which starred Virginia McKenna and Paul Scofield. He considerably extended his reputation in the 1960s with *The Greengage Summer* and, especially, *Alfie*, the prestige from which took him on to direct some of the high-profile James Bond movies — *You Only Live Twice*, *The Spy Who Loved Me* and *Moonraker*.

Gilbert was to prove that age was no barrier to making good movies. In his sixties, he scored unexpected success in 1983 with playwright Willy Russell's *Educating Rita*, starring Michael Caine, Julie Walters, Michael Williams and Maureen Lipman. Caine and Walters, along with Russell, were nominated for Oscars. Six years later he teamed once again with Russell to direct the incomparable *Shirley Valentine*, starring Pauline Collins, who received an Oscar nomination, and Tom Conti.

With such hit movies as these it is hardly surprising that Gilbert turned again to a stage adaptation when working out plans for his next picture. This time it was British writer Richard Harris' 'Stepping Out' which intrigued him. This was a show which had opened at London's Duke of York's Theatre in September 1984, starring Barbara Ferris, but less than three years later saw only seventy-two performances on Broadway before closing.

In the film version Liza was the recognized choice for the role of Mavis Turner, the 38-year-old harassed dance teacher with a generous spirit who fashions a group of mature no-hope tap tyros into a show-stopping troupe. Lewis Gilbert admitted later that he would not have done the movie if Liza could not have been cast in the key role. 'Mavis is a part only Liza could bring off. She is a world-class entertainer and what is special about her is her singing and dancing and that ineffable star quality,' he observed. He finished up as producer and director of this Paramount picture, with John Dark as co-producer, Bill Kenwright as executive producer, Danny Daniels as choreographer, and Peter Matz responsible for the musical score.

Gilbert's idea of doing *Stepping Out* was a godsend for Liza, who by now must have given up all hope of Hollywood, for there was every sign that she would be left to flounder in cinema's wasteland for ever. Sadly, she was the ultimate example of the negative side of an abundant talent too versatile for its own good. She sang, danced and projected a unique intensity and presence on the big screen. She had proved herself as a dramatic actress and comedienne. She was always impeccably professional when filming and had never been a problem on the set. What she lacked was an individual focus sufficiently strong for Hollywood's decision-makers to see her in a blockbuster role for the modern screen; to them she was stuck in the mould of a song-and-dancer. And, of course, by the late 1980s she had been around for quite some time and was by no means considered a contemporary talent.

But all this was shrugged aside by Lewis Gilbert. He was well into his seventies when the movie began shooting and experienced enough to realize that not all movies can or should be box-office blockbusters. That was not the sole criterion for a man concerned with making good and significant pictures.

His quiet yet positive direction began to mould a potential winner from Harris's lively and entertaining screenplay which cleverly, and almost inconsequentially, also contained gems of real pathos. Liza was excited about making another movie and reportedly jubilant at doing another musical. She worked hard to polish her tap-dancing skills and relished playing a storyline which gave her an integral part within a very talented cast which included Julie Walters and Shelley Winters. According to Jane Krakowski, who takes the part of Lynne, a petite young nurse who finds dance class a welcome break from the tensions and dolefulness of the wards, Liza considered the movie a cooperative effort, and insisted it was for the dance 'ensemble' and not merely a showcase vehicle for Liza Minnelli. Liza was irritated by press reports and comment that *Stepping Out* was her screen comeback, although after such a long absence it is not surprising that many critics were labelling it just that.

The very nature of the picture put it out of bounds for any kind of award. Nor was it ever likely to excite modern movie-goers sufficiently to make a startling impact at the box office. Nonetheless, it was to be a superbly beguiling, refreshingly innocent movie, with lots of vitality, good music, rhythmic toe-tapping and clever, well-timed moments of choice humour. The nearest the film would come to the vogue for four-letter words would be Liza's own choice remark, when teaching the elements of success for a dance team. 'Remember the three Ts when facing an audience,' she told them, 'teeth, taps and tits.'

The film centres around a weekly local dance class held in an unwelcoming church hall in downtown Buffalo, and is touching in both its storyline and individual character portrayals. Liza, as Mavis Turner, is a former chorus girl who gave up her chance of the big time to be with an egocentric guitar player, and tries to instil some kind of rhythm, style, teamwork and, yes, even the merest sniff of ambition, into a disparate assortment of learner hoofers. The ten dollars a lesson she receives for her pains is supplemented by stints as a singer in a club where her guitarist boyfriend plays.

The only man in Mavis' class of eight is the painfully shy, bespectacled Geoffrey, played faultlessly by Bill Irwin, who nonetheless becomes the romantic object of class colleague Andy ('long' for Ann), as she later explains to a nosey Vera (Julie Walters). Vera is the vexing, sneaky, insensitive, interfering British-born middle-class snob with a manic obsession for gossip and cleanliness and who never misses a chance to put herself above the others to score a point.

We quickly see the sort of person Vera is when she sweeps in as a newcomer to the class in clothes hardly befitting a dance rehearsal in a dusty hall. 'Excuse me, is this the tap class?' she enquires in a cringingly contrived attempt at an upper-crust accent, which elicits the retort from gum-chewing American extrovert Sylvia, played by Robyn Stevan: 'Oh my God, it's Princess Di.' Having decided to join, she automatically takes her place in prime position at the front of the class to the quiet annoyance of the others, until diplomatically moved to the back by Liza.

Over the following weeks of lessons, Vera gratuitously adopts a special role for herself, emptying ashtrays, tidying up, cleaning the windows and sills . . . and always decked in yellow rubber gloves, even when wearing a leopard skin jumpsuit. She puts up no smoking notices and complains about the rude graffiti scrawled on the loo walls. 'It's not us, it's the cub scouts,' jokes one of the girls. But it seems to satisfy the patronizing Vera.

The others in the class are Maxine (Ellen Greene) who, despite her style and provocative personality, is somewhat insecure and vulnerable; Andy (Sheila McCarthy), already mentioned, who is plain, thin, shy and, astonishingly when it is revealed later in the movie, is married to a domineering husband who beats her when he feels like it; Dorothy (Andrea Martin), an anxious librarian who lives with her ageing mother and suffers from pollen allergy, blowing her nose and sneezing all the time; Rose (Carol Woods), a large, happy, black lady who sees dance class as an escape from the kitchen sink and a nagging husband; and as already mentioned, Sylvia, a short curvaceous brunette with a penchant for bright, outrageous clothes.

All turn in first-rate performances, as does the veteran actress Shelley Winters, who plays Mrs Frazer — first name Glenda — pianist to the class, who, we are led to believe by her long-suffering, resigned attitude, has seen and done it all before. She presumably can do with the pittance Mavis is able to pay her for playing the old upright for the class, yet gives the impression of coming from a much loftier background. 'She's kind of a busybody and a very proud senior citizen,' observed Winters about her character. 'She's always making comments that the girls can't dance but then she begins to hope they really will succeed. It's like a group therapy lesson in tap dancing.' She is also stubborn and at times uncooperative. At one point she plays the music far too fast and is told so by Mavis. When she plays it again it is so ridiculously slow the class stumble all over the place, unable to dance to the now laboured tempo. Corrected again, she hesitates a moment, slams down the piano lid and walks off in a huff. Mavis has to be extra nice to coax her back.

At first it is just a dance class, a local diversion from routine, a bright shaft of sunlight to add a few moments of movement and sparkle to otherwise dull or disappointing lives.

We see the class practising their steps at home, in the kitchen, in a hospital ward, surreptitiously in church, out in the park and, of course, when they meet together in class. For these mature students tap class also becomes a way of learning about relationships, hopes and dreams. Despite the sometimes ramshackle organization behind the lessons, Mavis is an expert dancer and a good teacher. In one of the film's reflective moments she confides to one of her pupils: 'I always wanted to be a dancer and I still miss the profession . . . I did a lot of big shows, mostly in the chorus, and got to understudy the star who got sick and went on . . . for a week. I killed 'em . . . even auditioned for Bob Fosse once!'

'What happened?' comes the sympathetic response.

'Fell in love,' says Mavis in a rare defeated moment. But the unexpected chance comes for all of them to respond to one another and a new collective challenge when the class is given the opportunity to perform at a local Centre for Performing Arts at a big charity event. All the local dance academies have been invited and the story gains pace as the class goes into panic overdrive at the thought of performing on a real stage in front of a real audience; and in comparison with others! The result is exhilarating as Mavis tells them they can do it and gives them the confidence to believe it.

Above all it is a relaxed, enjoyable picture and, released at a time when

Hollywood seemed to be increasingly obsessed with violence and sex, the 'feel good' factor was well emphasized. While the characters are finely drawn, each a cameo in itself, there are no heavy messages to clutter up the plot or the fun. There are many choice interludes, some joyously surprising. At one point Mavis and Mrs Frazer, who often arrive for class together, are a little late for rehearsal and the normally hesitant, painfully-inhibited Geoffrey, who carries his tap shoes in a paper bag, descends on the piano and with remarkable abandon pounds out an outstanding boogie beat, to the open-mouthed astonishment of the class and his own confusion when Mavis and Mrs Frazer suddenly arrive.

It is Geoffrey, again, who bursts out of character with a superb right to the jaw, almost breaking his hand in the process, when the husband of Andy, with whom he has struck up an endearingly platonic friendship, threatens to prevent his wife from taking part in the concert. But understandably some of the best parts are down to Liza. A highlight of the film is when she is working out some of the steps while waiting for the class to arrive for rehearsal. Shafts of sun are streaming through the fanlight and against a background of mirrors her contemplative dance solo, created by Danny Daniels and lasting fully six minutes, shows her to be a most stylish performer with wonderful feeling and technique. She is smooth, shapely, expressive. Her sharpest critic couldn't have asked for more.

The film brings in snatches of established musical standards like 'Beyond the Blue Horizon', 'Isn't it Romantic' and the famous Frank Loesser, Hoagy Carmichael number 'Heart and Soul', but once again it is Liza who concentrates minds with some of her best singing on film with the old blues classic 'Mean to Me', which is a recurring musical theme in the picture.

Despite her insistence that *Stepping Out* was a team job, Liza of course is the star of the piece and she turns in a competent, even inspired performance. She seemed so naturally at ease in this song-and-dance situation. The story, script and content could have been created for her specifically.

She pitches the character just right — the smoking, enthusiastic, warm-hearted Mavis trying to scrape a living through teaching her class and singing at occasional nightclub gigs while at the same time trying unsuccessfully to hold on to the man she loves. She is not well-off and plainly down-at-heel — her team presents her with new tap shoes at an after-show party because they have noticed that she rehearses in a pair of old boots which she passes off as being 'comfortable' — but she wins the respect, loyalty and total support of her class by her sympathetic nature, understanding, genuine concern for them as individuals and her inspiration.

When things go wrong in class she often hides their mistakes under the false admission that she perhaps did not explain something clearly enough or that it was her fault, thus giving a boost to their confidence. As the time of the show approaches Lynn asks if they might each be allowed to do something individual as part of the routine, explaining when Mavis rejects the suggestion, that it isn't just her idea, some of the others had been thinking the same thing.

For once Mavis reacts angrily, unable to conceal her hurt feelings that they, lacking experience and limited on skill, should even consider changing the routine she has carefully worked out for them with due regard to their obvious limitations and lack of experience. She storms off. The earlier bloody-minded Mrs Frazer (Glenda), shows she has a heart after all and, realizing that they have badly hurt Mavis' feelings, goes off to comfort her, calling angrily to the class as she goes: 'I hope you're proud of yourselves.' What the class has no means of knowing, of course, is that Mavis' uncharacteristic outburst has been prompted by her boyfriend who has selfishly hot-footed it to Los Angeles in pursuit of a dubious gig, assuming that Mavis would immediately up-roots and go with him and giving no thought to her feelings or commitments. When Mavis returns to the class, consoled by Mrs Frazer and once again composed, she says her outburst was unforgivable, that she is sorry and that it won't happen again.

At the concert the team do well for

part-timers with little experience and, as the Mavis Turner Tappers, stumble and falter their way through the old tune 'Happy Feet', resplendent in smart jacket outfits topped and tailed with straw boaters and white shoes. Mavis is delighted and says how proud she is of them all, hugging and kissing them as she goes round the group. More important is that their enthusiasm and spirit strike such a special chord with the audience that they become the most popular dance studio with a guaranteed return engagement the following year. Mavis' personal spirit and example is heart-warming and as Liza was to explain later: 'There are times in one's life when one is gripped with a curious bravery; when all your instincts tell you to move in a new and unknown direction even though it may scare you. When you act on those instincts and move forward despite the fear . . . that's stepping out.'

The film, shot largely in Toronto, with only exteriors authentic Buffalo, seems to have been a happy experience for the players, though there were one or two poignant moments. Making the picture revived memories of a personal cross which Liza was having to bear. Mavis becomes unintentionally pregnant just prior to the end of a long relationship, and has a baby — unlike the real-life Liza, denied the child she had wanted so much.

It was also during the shooting that Julie Walters learned that her daughter, Maisie, then only two, had developed leukaemia and Julie decided to cut down on her professional work programme in order to look after her. After initial treatment came the trauma of a relapse, but more treatment helped mother and daughter to battle on bravely, with the result that a later medical assessment has given an optimistic 80 per cent chance of complete recovery for Maisie.

Liza was later to describe the experience of learning about Julie's and Maisie's problem as horrendous, but said that the cast were all inspired by Julie's strength in such a devastating situation. Liza recalled the earlier sequence in the film (already described) where her character remembers lost opportunities and dances alone and beautifully in the practice hall.

She explained that when she learned about Maisie she brought that dance forward in the shooting schedule because she wanted to do it right then. 'That was for Julie. I danced for Julie,' she told *Daily Mirror* show-business editor Hilary Bonner. As Miss Bonner reminded her readers: 'The remark may seem stagey. But Liza is totally sincere. You have to remember Hollywood runs through her veins.'

Stepping Out ends on a musical high with the troupe back again a year later at the Centre for Performing Arts to receive a tremendous ovation. Mavis arrives as a proud mum pushing her baby buggy; Mrs Frazer, preening like a peacock and resplendent in a long evening gown, is ensconced at the grand piano in the pit; and the Tappers, having become a very talented group under Mavis' sensitive tuition, and this time with canes and toppers and featuring Mavis Turner out front, go through a glorious six-minute routine, excluding encores, to the song specially composed for the picture by John Kander and Fred Ebb, 'Stepping Out'. It is a fitting, triumphant testimony to the simple yet powerful human instincts which drive people to accomplishments normally considered beyond their means. In a memorable picture it is interesting to pick out the clever way the troupe gradually develop from heavy-footed, raw, unbalanced and unskilled no-hopers to the confident, well-drilled, stylish and rhythmic toe-tappers we applaud at the end. Gilbert himself would later reveal that they were all mainly actors and not dancers. And on this occasion, in her singing, mannerisms and dialogue asides, Liza is sometimes so much like Judy it is almost uncanny.

In her private life also, it wasn't difficult to understand that Liza was her mother's daughter. Shortly after making *Stepping Out* she announced her divorce from Mark Gero; her third divorce. The marriage had been winding down for some time and, if her friends and supporters greeted the matrimonial severance with dismay and sorrow, Liza displayed no such regrets. She confessed that, although they had been married for twelve years, their lives had been falling apart, and the only positive thing to do was to call it a day. She showed just how successfully she had shrugged off the emotional frailty of her family heritage and any possible effects of post-clinic syndrome when she declared: 'There is reality. There is nothing I can do about yesterday, and who knows what is going to happen tomorrow. But today, I can do something.' To that extent she saw her divorce as a success.

Stepping Out brought Liza hot-foot to Britain for a royal world premiere at the Empire, Leicester Square, with the Princess of Wales as guest of honour. The film, released in 1991 and running 110 minutes, wasn't badly mauled by the critics, nor did it make any great or lasting impact with the general run of movie-goers. The *Daily Mail* probably had it about right when they reported: 'Liza and Julie sprinkle their magic on a musical tale.'

But the picture was a triumph for the veteran director Lewis Gilbert who, in 1990, after recently celebrating his seventieth birthday, was selected to receive the Michael Balcon Award, the highest honour of the British Academy of Film and Television Arts (BAFTA). This was presented by Princess Anne for his outstanding contribution to British cinema in a career which spanned more than six decades.

For Minnelli fans it was more than enough that Liza was back with a film and for them *Stepping Out* scored triumphantly for its toe-tapping rhythms, good ballads and swinging music — not to mention its non-defeatist storyline. Even among less partisan picture-goers and the critics with the sharpest points to their pencils, this transatlantic offering was widely considered to be the best thing Liza had done since *Cabaret*.

13

First-name Terms with the World

HAVING been born between 19 February and 20 March, Liza Minnelli is a Piscean. Those born under the sign of the fish are said to be less worldly than people born under the other eleven signs. There is also, according to the stars, a good chance that they will be intuitive, emotional and creative; highly compassionate, loving and sensitive to others. Pisceans, some assessments claim, find it almost impossible to conform to any set patterns of living and organization eludes them.

Liza probably relates reasonably closely to much of the above, but the broad definition fails specifically to pick up on her love of dogs, her near-obsessive appetite for hard work, or the way she tends to lose husbands but clings passionately to friends.

It was in Puerto Rico, in February

1969, that Liza collected her first dog, which she called Ocho, and which has been variously described as a 'shaggy mutt' and a 'bath-mat dog'. She once said, presumably after it had become acclimatized to living with Liza, that it only ate steak and caviare. Three years later, two more dogs joined the Minnelli family, a miniature Schnauzer called Emelina and another mongrel which she christened Pookie. During the time she was with Rex Kramer he bought her a couple of miniature poodles which she called Sophie and Lucy, but Ocho, after spending some time on Kramer's grandparents' ranch in Arkansas, where Liza often used to visit, departed in 1974 when she was adopted by a friend of Liza's in Brazil. But that same year, while Liza was in Mexico for three months shooting *Lucky Lady*, she befriended a tiny stray pup, which she called Claire. Her love of dogs, in the plural, and her inability to resist almost any dog with a pleading face, particularly a stray, led to the inevitable. With her film commitments completed she returned home with another dog, a black cocker spaniel pup called Cuchilla. Over the years Liza built up quite a collection of dogs and somehow, despite obvious problems of travel, would often have at least one with her wherever she was staying. Lilly joined the team when Liza saw her in a shop window and found her irresistible. Liza spoke enthusiastically about the three-year-old Cairn terrier and explained that when she took Lilly with her to Sweden she ran into trouble with the authorities. The thought of having to put her into quarantine was too much for Liza to contemplate, so she chartered a private jet and had the latest recruit to her dog team flown over to a friend in Paris.

Curiously enough, Liza's canine connection is strongly indicated through Chinese astrology, where every year belongs to an animal and those who are born in that year have the animal's characteristics. There are twelve animals which vary from tiger, buffalo and monkey to dragon, horse and even rooster. The chart shows that the year 1946, when Liza was born, belongs to — the dog! And the characteristics of the dog in Chinese astrology are: well-mannered, industrious, domesticated, but obstinate, egocentric and bad at planning. But maybe they shouldn't be taken too literally!

When Liza was filming *Stepping Out* in Toronto she shared her seventeenth-floor hotel suite with Lilly, and it was in that same suite in mid-1991, with Lilly once again ensconced, that an interview for *Premiere* magazine with film critic Jay Scott was held. A few moments earlier, while in the streets of Toronto, Liza had indirectly given the clue to another strong feature of her character: the value she places on friendships — with humans. Her presence in Toronto had excited beyond expectation that normally blasé town and Scott had wondered if being the object of such intense attention was not scary. 'Not when I'm with someone,' said Liza as they walked only yards away from a truck driver who had just slammed on the brakes and screamed 'Hey Liza!' and then gawked as she waved back. Liza admitted that when she's alone it is a bit scary, but explained that it has been going on so long she was used to it. But the truck driver's response to seeing her had sparked a significant memory. Informed Liza: 'A friend of mine not in show business said to me, "You're on a first-name basis with the world".' That statement says much about her character and personality and is indicative of her ability to forge deep and solid friendships which she nurtures and values, often for much of her life; friendships which are not devalued by arising out of their association with her work, as they often do.

Liza often gives the impression of living for the moment — one day at a time and all that — yet, perhaps surprisingly, also appears to place a solid value on friendships which are long-standing. Some of the most enduring friendships go back to her mother's and father's time. Kay Thompson was so close to Liza's parents that when she became her godmother and took her duties seriously, Liza was more than willing to do her part in forming a sustained friendship which has not faltered over the years. Thompson always seems to have been close to the core of Liza's life, ready to step in when her help and support was wanted most.

During the traumatic days following Judy's death it was Kay Thompson who was arguably closest of all to Liza, being an enormous help both practically and emotionally. A few years later, when Liza married Jack Haley Jnr and went to live in Jack's ranch-style house in the hills overlooking Los Angeles, Kay Thompson moved in to Liza's New York apartment to live there. She also became a kind of personal manager, advising and helping Liza with many aspects of her career. Incidentally, Thompson, a successful performer, talented singer, writer and actress, was also the author of the fictional heroine Eloise. The first book in the Eloise series was published in 1955 and is said to be based principally on the escapades of Liza.

Many of those who have shared Liza's deep and lasting friendship have also been her greatest influences. Sammy Davis Jnr was always an inspiration — she would call Sammy for advice long after she became a recognized star — and so to a lesser degree has been Frank Sinatra. Liza remembers with amusement her first audition when she was sixteen. She called

Davis to see what she should sing. Sing something fast, sing something slow and sing something they know, he advised her. As *The Sunday Times* columnist Lesley White once reported: 'It was more than professional counsel, it was to turn into a way of life. More than her voice or her looks or her dancing talent, Minnelli's appeal is the link she provides with straight razzmatazz.' It made no difference to the special bond which existed between them that, on another occasion, Sammy gave her advice which would have sent her off in the wrong direction; or that she chose to disregard his advice. The time in question was when she had the chance to step in temporarily for the illness-stricken Gwen Verdon in the hit Broadway musical, *Chicago*. Sammy said she was already a star in her own right and it would be wrong for her to perform a deputy's role. 'Let the understudy take over,' he advised. But for Liza it was too good an opportunity to miss. She followed her own instincts and scored an enormous triumph. Next day her dressing room was filled with flowers with a small card attached. 'Anyone can make a stupid mistake,' was Sammy's apologetic message.

After more than thirty years she is still proud to call Marvin Hamlisch her friend. Much of her success, she will eagerly acknowledge, has to do with the close and continuing professional relationship she has enjoyed since *Best Foot Forward* with the song-writing partnership of Kander and Ebb; Fred Ebb particularly. Almost everything she has done, the significant milestones in her career, the most outstanding triumphs, all have been in close association with Ebb, once described as her closest male friend.

As composer and lyricist, the John Kander and Fred Ebb team must be one of the most under-rated in the business. Their record in the theatre is impressive enough, extending from *Flora, the Red Menace* and *Cabaret* to *Kiss of the Spider Woman, the Musical* and including *The Happy Time*, *Chicago*, *The Act* and *The Rink*. Their film successes have included *Cabaret*, *New York, New York*, *Funny Lady*, *Kramer vs Kramer* and *Stepping Out*;

while for television they have achieved perhaps even more success: *Baryshnikov on Broadway*, *An Early Frost*, *Ol' Blue Eyes is Back* with Frank Sinatra, *Gypsy in My Soul* with Shirley MacLaine; and (all with Liza), *Liza With a Z*, *Goldie and Liza Together* (with Goldie Hawn) and *Liza in London*. Their contribution to Liza's outstanding impact over the years as a 'live' entertainer in concert halls, theatres and clubs all over the world is one of the most remarkable liaisons in show business, with Ebb's personal value as director, and often creator, of many of her most impressive stagings, being incalculable. In song-writing terms alone their contribution to Liza's success is prodigious. How is it possible to value just three of their prolific output: 'Cabaret', 'New York, New York' and 'Stepping Out'?

It is not surprising therefore that Liza was strongly featured in a well-deserved 'tribute' programme to Kander and Ebb called *Sing Happy* in New York City in November 1978. This special night was described as a huge reunion and expression of love for two very special men, and on hand to join in the celebration were Chita Rivera, Gwen Verdon, Cy Coleman, Joel Grey, Jerry Herman and many others. Liza sang and danced solo and later joined Rivera and Verdon for 'Keeping it Hot' and 'Pain'.

Other examples of the friendships Liza so values are musician Bill La Vorgna, whom she has known since she was a child and has worked with for almost as long, the late Bob Fosse, and Shirley MacLaine, who was her mother's friend. Halston, too, became a close friend. Liza described him as being very sensitive and very strong and she considered he had done a marvellous fashion job on her, being undaunted by her very broad shoulders. 'He gave me a style and my own look,' she once said. He certainly encouraged her into a stronger and more appealing dress-sense, both on and off the stage, to such effect that in 1972 she was named as one of the ten best-dressed women in the world. She has acknowledged Elizabeth Taylor as a friend for more years that she cares to remember. It says something about the woman that she still probably considers one of her best friends to be Pam Rhinehardt, an unknown with no connections with show business, but who was her matron of honour when she married Peter Allen.

It also appears significant that she has retained the friendship of all three former husbands and of many of the men with whom she once had a relationship. In almost all cases there is this curious crossover between the private and professional in her friendships. She seems almost incapable of having a love affair that is not also a professional relationship. This has carried on to the present time when her latest friend, Billy Stritch, is also her current musical director. She has the ability, when romance fades, to salvage a special kind of friendship which extends over the years.

She also lists her family as being among her best friends. Liza does not consider this to be a diminution of their status, just the reverse in fact, and over recent years she and Lorna have become very close friends as well as kindred souls in show business. When dates and commitments permit they will often attend functions together, sometimes taking Joey along with them; and they generally welcome the opportunity to appear together professionally. In television interviews she welcomes the opportunity to explain that her sister Lorna is her best friend and appears humble and pleased that they are so close.

A more transient inspiration and friend was film director Martin Scorsese during the late 1970s and early 1980s, principally through their work together on *New York, New York*, and *The King of Comedy*. He also worked with Liza when staging her Broadway show, *The Act*. His special sense of creativity and his close identification with, and skilful projection of, the American way of life, would undoubtedly strike a special chord with Liza.

Whether, as the astrology charts indicate for a Piscean, Liza is 'less worldly than those people born under the other eleven signs', is certainly open to question. Of less doubt, however, is the old saying about Tuesday's child being full of grace. She may sometimes sit awkwardly, and move around the stage with abundant energy, and her posture and deportment may at times be questionable, but when the need is there no-one walks or dances with more grace. Her capacity for hard work is what often impresses the most experienced film director and anyone involved with her live performances. She says without hesitation that she enjoys the process of rehearsal best of all in her life as an entertainer, which is perhaps a little unusual in the business. It is the steady creation of something out of nothing which attracts her and leads her to be unstinting in rehearsal. Once that job is done she will carry her capacity for work into her personal appearance schedules, as the original draft of Liza Minnelli concert dates for 1993 amply proved. Only one month out of the twelve was left free of projected commitments and some months like January and February indicated a near congestion of performances: January (1 – 3) Las Vegas, (9) Stamford and (29) Pasadena. February (3 – 7) Las Vegas, (13) Melbourne, (14 – 15) Ft Meyers, (17 – 18) Daytona Beach, (20 – 21) Clearwater, (22 – 23) Sarasota and (25 – 28)

Ft Lauderdale. Projected dates throughout June: (1 – 7) New York, (9 – 13) Toronto, Canada, (16 – 20) Washington DC and (23 – 27) Montreal, Canada were with Charles Aznavour, while the whole of September was taken up with a planned tour of South America.

Those who know her best would be able to agree that she was intuitive, emotional and creative. Peter Allen once said that she has the ability to believe totally in a situation at any given time, which is what Judy had too. He added: 'She's incredibly smart and intuitive, but she never intellectualizes anything. She'll push down her natural intellect to work with her emotions every time.' He also pointed out that she has good taste and uses the right people, and that her philosophy is to be a moving target. Her intellectual savvy was apparent before she reached her twenties.

There is in the public mind a brash veneer to the Minnelli personality and this can be misleading. She is more sophisticated than a casual opinion would suggest and her intellect is sharp, yet substantial. This comes through smoothly in the television interviews she gives, where she reveals herself to be a thinking and articulate individual. She is also subtly opportunist and clever when required to promote the interests of her activities, particularly during television interviews. Nobody does it with a greater degree of skill and understanding of the medium. Many of these interviews are arranged when the focus is on her through the release of a new film, or when she is in town with a new show. To re-run film clips of interviews which took place at the time of *Stepping Out* is a revelation. It is perhaps surprising just how deftly she can turn an interview back to what she sees as the focus of it all (in this case *Stepping Out*) — even with the most experienced of interrogators, and when the interviewer has moved the conversation into areas such as her turbulent childhood, her earlier drink and drug dependency or her failed marriages. She will manoeuvre the interview back to her new film or her new show with a clever, natural and almost imperceptible link which gives not the slightest offence and requires no forced assertion. Her eyes light up and she uses her hands a lot in talking, particularly when in her stride during an interview, but there is still the underlying impression of vulnerability which can mask her inner toughness and strength of character.

In some respects the dividing line between the real Liza and her stage image is deceptively thin. In other ways the private and the public Liza are two distinct people. Journalists will tell you that she often appears for interviews showing little if any makeup. All the paint and the glitz is for when she is performing. 'In daily life I'm content to go out in my scrubbed look,' she once explained, adding: 'I don't mind too much being photographed plain. I'm not an image. I'm a woman, and the public accepts all facets of me, I think. I don't compete with anyone else and I don't compete with myself.' Someone once said that in spite of her star image, her fame and her obvious wealth, she looks abnormally normal.

The emotional and creative aspects of her character can be identified many times in her performances and also in her comments. Her admiration for Aznavour, for instance, has much to do with those two qualities. She will tell you even now that when she was seventeen and saw Aznavour sing a song for the first time it was a considerable emotional experience. She found it absorbing that when he sang he acted. 'It was like a little movie,' she explained. 'Each piece had a life of its own.' This is often her reason for singing the songs she does, songs which might not be first choice for the public, but which she is drawn to because they carry a message or have some underlying meaning. There is a poet within her. Words have always been important in her life, and at one time she would spend many off-duty hours producing verse. When Sammy Davis was ill and Liza was in London, she sent him a fax every day, ending with a poem.

She is concerned to relate specifically to situations and audiences. When asked by a young audience what her ambition was, she didn't respond with a grand gesture such as 'I always wanted to be a star' or 'I knew from three years old that I wanted to go on the stage'.

She recognized the emotional desires of young girls and related to them with shrewd perception: 'My ambition was to be sixteen,' she said light-heartedly. 'It seemed like it would take forever.'

There is this plaintive quality to her personality, yet she has been toughened by the hard times she has faced in show business. Her outward personality often hides a keen sense of humour, not for the formal telling of standard jokes, but more for impromptu witticisms brought in casually during conversation arising from real incidents. Her humour is quietly penetrating as she tells you about the weeks the troupe spent in dance rehearsal for *Stepping Out*, explaining that the film was about discovering themselves as individuals, their inner strengths, and the positive elements of working together in something new. 'When your feet bleed it bonds you,' she explains. She likes to wear black because she is a dancer and black is generally good for rehearsals. And anyway, 'my weight goes up and down and black hides all that.'

The humour eases through a voice which is at most times gentler than you might expect and occasionally seems to break slightly. She then becomes more animated, explaining, with eyes glowing, how on the set in Germany they affectionately called *Cabaret* the 'nifty Nazi follies', and describing her first adventure through Checkpoint Charlie into East Berlin as 'quite an experience' because she had only ever before seen the horses' behinds at the Brandenburg Gate.

If there is one thing that Liza Minnelli regrets it would probably be that she was not around during the heyday of the film musical. But she will tell you that she is not one to harbour regrets or dwell on the darker aspects of life, though she did once point out in a disappointed, reflective tone that Judy didn't live to see her success in *Cabaret*. After Halston died an interviewer said to her how regrettable it was that he was no longer around. She thought for a second and then, quietly with a smile, said: 'Yes, but it was so great that he was here at all.' When Sammy Davis was desperately ill and she was asked how he was, her response was sympathetic and gentle, but not defeatist: 'Oh, he's all right' she said slowly, then: 'He's been better' (leaving no-one in doubt about the critical nature of his condition), and then, more optimistically, 'but he's okay.'

Sometimes, in career terms, she gives the impression of wanting to be all things to all people and this can spill over into non-professional life. She is a self-proclaimed hopeless romantic, but at the same time is practical and philosophical, a text-book Piscean in fact. She clings to the positive images of her mother and father and, despite what she might say, seems to be more comfortable in singing the older songs. Yet somehow she seems curiously able to turn this kind of nostalgia into a positive element in her life which is not out of tune with the emphasis on fun and reality which is so important to her. She likes rehearsals because they are fun. She enjoys being with Lorna because she is 'funnier than anyone I know'. She enjoyed *Stepping Out* not so much because it was a musical film, but because it was a musical about real people.

One of the fascinations about Liza is that she is a colourful and dynamic individual in a show-business world where more pedestrian personalities have become the fashion. Another is that despite her superstar status you can still actually pay to see her 'live'; this in an age when the remoteness of many celebrities because of the big screen and television is virtually total. As a fan you can still get close to her. The 'Hi, Liza' factor is still very much a reality.

14

Liza . . . Live!

ON Friday, 12 March 1993 Liza Minnelli was forty-seven and if she looked somewhat older than she did when she made *Cabaret* more than twenty years before, there was no doubt that in passing through the time zones she had managed somehow to dodge much of the damaging fallout. She looked better that she had done many times in the past. The face looked friendlier, more sensitive, the features less angular. The physique was still admirably shapely. Temperamentally she was perhaps more controlled and balanced than at any time in her life.

Of course the passing years would bring the inevitable emotional scars. Many of those famous Hollywood names she had known as friends, though from a previous generation, had passed on. Her co-stars in *A Matter of Time* in 1976 had both died, Boyer in 1978 when, two days after the death of his wife and grief-stricken, he committed suicide; and Ingrid Bergman. She had grieved when her close friend and confidante for many years from the fashion world, Halston, died. And her beloved father was also gone.

Another great blow was delivered in the summer of 1990 with the death at sixty-four of Sammy Davis Jnr. All her life she had remained close to Sammy. He was the benevolent 'uncle' during the time her mother was alive, a devoted friend and inspiration when she began to climb the ladder of show business. It was Sammy who would help her when she was down, and boost her confidence with encouraging remarks when, as a star in her own right, she sometimes found herself doubting her own ability. As she herself put it: 'He taught me to say "Yes I can". By that I mean his determination and his independence.'

So it was no surprise that Liza should be there to head a major charity tribute to the great entertainer held at the Royal Albert Hall, London, on 23 June 1992. Promoted as *Liza and Friends in a*

Tribute to Sammy Davis Jnr, this single concert, with Princess Di as guest of honour, would raise more than £500,000 for the Royal Marsden Cancer Appeal.

Among the artists paying their respects to the memory of Sammy were Tom Jones, Cliff Richard, Jerry Lewis and Charles Aznavour. Joan Collins put in an appearance, as did Lionel Blair, an ageing Donald O'Connor, and Liza's sister, Lorna. However, as so often is the case with show business tributes, the sentiments and emotion of the occasion seemed to get in the way of full-blooded artistry and slick organization. That's not to imply any criticism of American Express, whose sponsorship enabled Liza's idea for the concert to go ahead. On the contrary, their initiative was commendable and Sammy himself would have been well pleased that his memory was being so magnificently observed.

At one point the amplification screeched momentarily; Cliff Richard and Tom Jones sang competently, though their contribution seemed oddly detached; and although Lorna Luft belted out

'I Gotta be Me' in a semblance of Garland tradition — and for her pains was given precedence over Liza by one London critic (which was surely bending over too far backwards to be equitable to Judy's kids) — her delivery, though sincere enough, was lumpy and laboured. Liza too had sung better. Her voice seemed at times ragged and a little under strength, as though she was on the verge of a cold, or suffering slight voice strain. But she cantered around the stage in a maelstrom of activity with songs and banter which was typically Minnelli. Her genuine feelings for Sammy were obvious, and some of the reminiscences painful, but she kept her emotions in check and in all it was a happy, swinging occasion of dedication.

Liza took over for the entire second half and, attractively costumed in a dark trouser suit and a white full-sleeved shirt, opened with the meaningful 'Come Back to Me'. Then off came the jacket and, looking slightly less vulnerable as she warmed up, sang other songs interspersed with anecdotes about Sammy, who obviously had held a very special place in her affections as a mixture of best friend, father figure and inspirational coach.

Despite the underlying sadness of the occasion, there were deft touches of self-deprecating humour, for which Liza is well-known, though they were slotted in neatly without warning and could easily have been missed by the audience. One such example was when she emerged in a smart black dress, short enough to display her dimpled knees, and a huge matching scarf. There was a pause as the audience quietened and then, swinging the scarf around her neck in mock deliberation in order to draw attention to the gesture, she said quietly: 'Sammy always said it was the effort that counts.'

There were old favourites like 'If I Ruled the World' and a medley of tuneful memories from the repertoire of Leslie Bricusse and Anthony Newley which included 'What Kind of Fool Am I' and 'Candy Man', both of which had been enormous hits for Sammy. But, from a musical standpoint, easily the most memorable segment of the entire programme came when she introduced her musical director, Billy Stritch. Said Liza: 'Meet someone who is very special to me, who has helped me to write the whole show and who is a great jazz singer . . . Mr Billy Stritch.' This young and enormously talented musician had been close to Liza since her marriage breakup from Mark Gero, even before perhaps, and now they showed just how inspirational is their professional partnership.

First came 'At Sammy's House', specially penned for the occasion by Fred Ebb, which ended with a rousing reprise with the extended last line, 'those wonderful nights, miraculous nights, at Sammy's House'. The evening continued with the coolest of jazz-interpreted standards with Stritch playing deft piano and sharing some of the vocals with Liza in a well-chosen selection which included all-time favourites like 'There Will Never Be Another You', 'Just You, Just Me', 'Fascinating Rhythm', 'Any Place I Hang My Hat is Home', even 'Chattanooga Choo Choo', 'Kansas City Here I Come' and 'Dream, When You're Feeling Blue'. While her voice has its flaws and her pitching can be unsteady, the standard Liza set with this selection leads one to wonder why she hasn't done more jazz ballads and big band standards during her career, as well as show numbers.

It is on occasions such as this that Liza, despite all her experience, still occasionally lapses into the ingenue of earlier years, showing us how the veteran trouper continues to be starry-eyed and almost overwhelmed by the association she has enjoyed since childhood with many of the legendary names of mainstream show business. It's as if she still cannot fully comprehend her good fortune in being dropped into such a galaxy of special people simply through the circumstances of her birth. Some critics who attended the tribute concert complained that she talked too much and thought the so-called old-hat showbiz corn had been overdone; but the audience certainly had no misgivings and loved her even more when, once over the delighted surprise of hearing a pre-recorded message from Frank Sinatra, the old Rat Pack legend announced that Liza Minnelli would be the first recipient of the 'Sammy' award, with Jerry Lewis handing over the statuette at the start of an emotional finale.

Liza's visit to London this time, memorable because of Sammy, was saddened by the announcement of the death from AIDS of her first husband, Peter Allen. Despite their divorce eighteen years before they had remained friends and, although his death was not a surprise to Liza, it was still a shock. In the intervening years Peter had built a strong reputation as a songwriter, producing hits for people like Melissa Manchester, Frank Sinatra, Olivia Newton-John and Rita Coolidge, though his biggest impact had been in 1981 with the song 'Best That You Can Do', which he co-wrote with Burt Bacharach, Carole Bayer Sager and Christopher Cross for, curiously enough, Liza's film *Arthur*. The song secured an Oscar.

Liza knew of Peter's illness and revealed that they had stayed close. It turned out that Peter, only forty-eight at the time of his death at San Diego County Hospital in California, had helped her prepare for Sammy's tribute show at the Royal Albert Hall. Said Liza: 'Even though he was ill he was still thinking about me and Sammy. Peter was a wonderful man. It's too startling and sad to face.'

It had been an altogether much happier occasion some nine months before, on 30 September 1991 when, back in Los Angeles, Liza had attended a special ceremony in Hollywood for the unveiling of the Liza Minnelli star on the famous Walk of Fame which stretches along Hollywood Boulevard. Liza and Billy Stritch arrived together in a luxury limo to be greeted by a host of her fans, some of whom had been getting in line since the previous night. The ceremony took place at 11.30 in the morning in front of the Hollywood Roosevelt Hotel, which itself has a long and celebrated history steeped in the traditions of Hollywood and its classic stars. A superb seated bronze of Charlie Chaplin adorns the lobby and never fails to capture attention.

Liza became the 1,939th star to be honoured on the Hollywood Walk of Fame. A press release covering the occasion announced: 'Minnelli, winner of three Tony awards, an Oscar, two Golden Globe awards and an Emmy, is one of the entertainment world's consummate performers. In film, on stage, and in television, Minnelli has won critical acclaim, recognition from her peers in show business and a multitude of fans.'

This happy occasion took place just four days before the release on 4 October of *Stepping Out*, and Liza's choreographer for the picture, Danny Daniels, was there to surprise Liza with a tap dance up and down the Walk of Fame in her honour. Liza, however, insisted on being the first person to step on her star after the ceremonial unveiling. Sister Lorna was there with her own toddler daughter, Vanessa, along with Joey, Jack Haley Jnr and Lee Minnelli, the widow of her late father. (Vincente had married Lee Anderson on 2 April 1980; Liza and Mark Gero had flown out to Beverly Hills for the ceremony and Liza was the Matron of Honour.) Liza's special 'star' day was also attended by Johnny Grant, the honorary mayor of Hollywood, and the marching band of the University of Southern California. She received a special certificate from the City of Los Angeles designating 30 September 1991 as 'Liza Minnelli Day'. The efforts and dedication of the Liza Minnelli international fan club helped to make this special event possible, and it was almost as big a day for them as for Liza herself, with club president Suzan Meyer there to represent her worldwide following in an official capacity.

The occasion had been slotted into Liza's customary hectic schedule of personal appearances which would include visits to New Jersey, New York, Las Vegas, Boston, Buffalo, San Carlos and Detroit. For her British public however, the big event was the release on 30 November 1992 of the video, CD and cassette under the title *Liza Minnelli 'Live' from Radio City Music Hall*, taped from her record-shattering engagement at the famous New York venue in April and May of the previous year. Billed as the 'performance of a lifetime' it certainly underscored the belief of a number of critics concerned more with objectivity than contrived journalistic angles, that in the early 1990s Liza Minnelli was at the very top of her form.

The show was spectacular, emotionally charged, clever, musical and, above all, outstandingly entertaining whether or not you watched as a devotee. Certainly Liza captured the attention and hearts of her vast audience, holding them spellbound with her third song, 'Sorry I Asked', about a woman trying to cope, when she holds a pause for four or five seconds, which seems an almost embarrassing eternity. It was a courageous thing to do, and one which few artists would have attempted. Even fewer would have got away with it.

The show opened with an up-tempo version of 'Teach Me Tonight' which Liza sang with typical gusto and, if the occasional note could have been cleaner and stronger, her powerhouse presence on stage came through instantly. From then on the ninety minutes of sheer entertainment was always vividly alive. She has great skill in varying the pace of her programme and proved just how adept she is in carrying her audience, switching arrestingly from one mood to another, singing, talking, moving, laughing. 'So What', from the original production of *Cabaret* — surely a magnanimous if justified gesture — was followed by the saucy 'Sara Lee' in which she moves into characteristic gestures and poses with arms and legs spread diagonally, and goes walkabout along the catwalk, a choice which brought her closer to her audience.

Typically, Liza used her songs to bring in pointed messages and tell interesting little stories about things that have happened to her and the people she has known in her life. Two numbers by Charles Aznavour ('I've been crazy about him all my life, not only as a performer, but as a writer; he writes about things other writers wouldn't touch'), provided a quiet, reflective interlude. 'There Is a Time' was handled partly in French, and in 'Quiet Love' she brought those expressive hands and fingers to work in sign language, for a time singing in a whisper, then shouting — and again her artistry and conviction allowed her to get away with it; and then her whole being was alive in the up-tempo 'Some

People' in which almost everything about her shook and moved.

The distinctive quality about Liza Minnelli is her ability to make cameos of everything she does; she acts every song, gives her whole being to every small facet of the programme, whether she is singing, talking, moving, looking, dancing, even pausing. The song 'Seeing Things' provided the opportunity for her to look back affectionately on her father. A big screen dropped down and a sequence of family snapshots showed Liza growing up with her father along with Vincente on his own at different stages of his lifetime, adding poignancy to an already touching delivery, with Liza explaining how magical her father was to her, what a very shy and humble man he was, and although most of her audience must have heard it all before, they seemed happy enough to hear it again as she informed them: 'I got my drive from my mother, but my dreams from my father.'

But there were informative points too. Many people must have been surprised when Liza explained that her father had spent four years as art director at Radio City Music Hall, and a selection of his costume design sketches was flashed up on the screen. As ever Liza seemed totally absorbed by the messages she presented and she honoured her father saying, 'I loved him very much and every single day I'm grateful that I'm seeing things his way,' linking up with the song title. The sequence ended with a picture on screen of father and daughter happily together, while on stage the watching and obviously moved Liza only just held on to her composure.

The show was a classy presentation from beginning to end, carefully modulated and cleverly executed. It opened with Liza as a lone silhouette in a white mini-raincoat designed by Isaac Mizrahi — a dramatic outfit she later wore to end the show — walking away from her audience, turning at the back of the stage where the lights picked her out while the darkened space around her worked gradually closer until it suddenly went black and the star of it all had gone. In between, the second half excelled even more convincingly than the first.

Dressed in a dazzling white shirt, black satin trousers with a brightly-coloured purple overskirt, Liza swung into 'Stepping Out', but was interrupted when first one female in the audience stood up to banter with her, then another, a third and so on, all claiming the right to go up on stage to be part of the number. It was a neat and amusing way of getting her twelve Demon Divas on stage before leading into a pulsating series of song-and-dance numbers all angled on the subject of men. In a long production number in the very best traditions of the Hollywood musical, which never faltered for a moment, Liza and her chorus-line zipped through twenty contrasting numbers. These ranged from 'Give Me Some Men', 'Some Day My Prince Will Come' and 'Mr Sandman' to 'The Bigger They Come the Harder They Fall' and 'Bewitched, Bothered and Bewildered', with Liza bringing the remarkable sequence to an end with an impressive solo performance of 'The Man I Love'.

Then, in a sequined top and black

tights, Liza led her team into a sensitive and atmospheric tribute to Bob Fosse, specially created for the concert by Fred Ebb and choreographer Susan Stroman. This sequence worked its way cleverly through 'Pack Up Your Troubles' and 'It's a Long Way to Tipperary' before leading without pause into the John Lennon number, 'Imagine', incorporating some nice chorus singing and a beautifully restrained ending. 'Here I'll Stay' was linked musically with 'Our Love is Here to Stay' — the latter bringing the greatest volume of spontaneous applause of the whole presentation because of its imaginative and individual interpretation — before moving back to 'Here I'll Stay', a tour-de-force finish to a sequence noted for its choreography and fine dancing.

Three show-stoppers increased the pace to end the show on an exciting and highly-charged peak. 'There's No Business Like Show Business' moved the finale off to a rousing start and this was followed by an extended reprise of 'Stepping Out', for which Liza changed from her simple black outfit into a dazzling red and white number. For this segment she was joined by the Demon Divas exhibiting an abundance of verve, delight, skill and sheer exuberance in a particularly long and arduous sequence which finished with a syncopated tap routine with traditional canes. Then at the very end there was the inevitable 'New York, New York', without which it is by now impossible for Liza to finish any of her performances. The concert was a huge triumph for everyone concerned and would stand out as a pinnacle of Liza's impressive concert career. The staging throughout was imaginative and smooth, the programme carefully conceived, the 'Mexican wave' final curtain-call was novel, and Liza looked as stunning as she has ever done in a body-hugging red leotard before she again donned the white mini-raincoat to close the show.

Given this performance, few would question Liza's reputation as one of the very top concert artists of our time. She appeared so at home in this kind of environment, on stage in a close one-to-one relationship with her audience; it is scarcely surprising if film-makers feel unnerved about the idea of pulling her away from a medium which she has so much made her own. 'Liza Live,' said the blurb, 'takes you on an unforgettable journey through a dazzling performance of storytelling, song and dance.' That just about tells it all. But for anyone looking for signs of a surge in Liza's fortunes as a movie actress, the early 1990s would be sadly disappointing. *Stepping Out* was again identified as a Minnelli typecast role by producers, as *New York, New York* had been and, in the pounding, repetitive world of rock and rap, musical pictures like these were still seen as a symbol of a bygone age, unless a clever theme or storyline could provide a new dimension. So after thirty years as a top celebrity performer, how does she fare in the dramatically different entertainment vista of the 1990s, as a person and as an artist?

To her credit, she has managed to avoid a fate similar to her mother's, though at one time she gave every impression of hurtling straight towards it. It is admirable that she has never lost the pride and love she had for her mother, when she could so easily have been sucked into the widespread and often lurid denouncements which attended Garland's final years. She never traded on her mother's reputation and, while the likeness was startlingly eerie and uncanny at the beginning, Liza has very much developed her own personality, becoming totally her own person.

She falls way behind her mother in the impact she has had in films. She has appeared in only eleven feature films in almost twenty-five years. Judy, by comparison, during her most prolific spell, shot through more than thirty pictures in a similar period. Time can play tricks, however, and to look back on Judy's pictures, even some of the better ones, is to appreciate just how much standards of acting have risen in motion pictures since that period often referred to as 'the glory days of cinema'.

And Hollywood is a far different place in the 1990s. There are fewer pictures being made than in Judy's day and hardly any which throw up roles of substance for female performers despite the age of so-called sexual equality.

Barbra Streisand was perhaps the first to articulate strongly this unhappy and demoralizing situation for top actresses. Others have denounced it, including Jane Fonda and the veteran Lauren Bacall. Liza undoubtedly has suffered from it. So critical is the situation that a recent Oscar committee was reportedly scraping around for contenders for the year's Best Actress category because while the talent is there, so few movie scripts had been written to project it. Younger emerging actresses are not protected from this disappointing situation. An example is Britain's Miranda Richardson, who in 1993 was seen in *Damage*, Louis Malle's film version of Josephine Hart's best-selling novel. She is dismissive about the six years since her last Hollywood hit role, complaining that after her big success with *Enchanted April* and *The Crying Game* she was only offered hellcat roles. She turned down the Glenn Close part in *Fatal Attraction* because it was so regressive and she didn't want to be known as someone who plays characters who stick scissors into people. The movieworld's recent predilection for sex and violence angled to a younger market hasn't helped.

Too much comparison between Liza and her mother, though still at times inevitable because of Garland's powerful persona and the many tragic circumstances of her life, is best avoided. Increasingly it is becoming meaningless. After all, it is almost twenty-five years since Judy died, and in that time there has been a revolution in life itself, which has affected the direction and positioning of entertainment in almost all its forms. Liza is her own woman, a celebrity in her own right, a dazzling and consummate performer in whatever medium she finds herself. These days she appears so completely in charge of her affairs and so emblematic of her craft and profession, that it seems she couldn't really have done anything other than go into show business. In cabaret and live performances on stage she is unchallenged by any other female performer. Perhaps that is the reason the film *Cabaret* was such a watershed in her career. But which came first? As long as twenty years ago she could rate a $60,000 fee for a week at one of the swank American nightspots. You would have to empty a much deeper purse these days before her agents would even bother to mention it to her. As someone once said, at an age when many performers are living in fifth-floor walk-ups, Liza was earning close to a million dollars a year. Yet it would be hard to find anyone who does more for charity where, particularly when one of her chosen areas is concerned, she is generous with her time and talent and has raised enormous sums.

Much of the support she gives is barely noticeable, being channelled on an organised basis through the international structure of her fan club. After a session with Liza, Suzan Meyer, president of 'Limelight on Liza', established 'Liza's Kids'. Explained Suzan: 'She truly appreciates all the gifts and flowers sent to her, but felt that the money could go to helping others less fortunate.' Nowadays, whenever a donation is made to 'Liza's Kids', a notification is sent to Liza.

She also gets involved with cooperative efforts, like a gala concert at the Universal Amphitheater in Los Angeles, to help raise funds for the AIDS project charity. Shirley MacLaine and Liza joined Elton John, Johnny Mathis, Barbra Streisand and many others in singing excerpts from Leonard Bernstein's hit musical, *West Side Story*. Other celebrities there included Natalie Cole, Billy Joel and Bianca Jagger.

Since she hit the big-time with *Cabaret* in 1972 she has never lost the ability to earn big money. She is known to be careful with money and has a sensible respect for what she earns. She appears to be well advised by professional people and over the years has invested wisely. She is said to own carefully-chosen tracts of land in key areas as part of her investments. She is a great traveller and loves being on the move, and has resolutely resisted the habit of many of her 'star' contemporaries who hide themselves away in a luxury pad in somewhere like Malibu, out of the limelight before their time. She loves New York, not just for what it means in terms of her success. Years ago she said she felt more at home in the big city and despite her early life in Hollywood, New York seems to be her spiritual home, where her heart is, close to the concert halls and live entertainment.

Nobody seems to work harder. Planning, preparing and giving concerts and cabaret performances all the time is a shattering commitment and she appears to be constantly on the move. She has emerged from her earlier waywardness a young-looking, fit and vibrant person, despite her chain-smoking, nail-biting and highly committed way of life. Fashionably she has never been a trend-setter. Her hairstyle has remained basically the same over the years, a few more spikes one time, a little longer another. But she manages during every engagement to emerge looking startling and stunning, often displaying those long legs to advantage. Where her art is concerned she is uncompromising in her standards and true to her own instincts. She is passionate about what she does. No-one can captivate an audience in quite the same way. She personifies entertainment and show business.

At forty-seven she instinctively relates musically to the days when the ballad and the big band were the mainstream of popular music for young people and, probably because of her parents, to the tinsel-town image of Hollywood, both of which were fading before she was even teenage. It irritates some critics that she still appears to derive her inspiration from the swinging days of Ella Fitzgerald, Nat King Cole and Tony Bennett. Yet she is not alone in this. Popular entertainers are usually caught within their time warp. Cliff Richard today is much the Cliff Richard of ten years ago. At eighty-five Stephane Grappelli plays jazz violin as he has done all his life. Sinatra, though an occasional working pensioner, isn't expected to begin vocalizing rap music. Indeed, Liza has perhaps done more than most by showing that she can make an impact on the pop scene with her success with the Pet Shop Boys those few years ago.

Meantime, the individual persona which Liza battled hard to establish from beneath the shadow of her mother has been comprehensively achieved. Not that Judy is forgotten. Far from it. Liza still refers to her as the best friend she ever had, but a long time ago cast out the residual melancholia which tends still to haunt Judy's memory for many people. Yet at the same time she is criticized for being over-sentimental, of trading on her late mother and father by talking about them in her act; indeed, by making them part of her act. Some critics say she carries exuberance too far, using visual excesses of gesture, audience relationship, movement on stage and nostalgia to cloak a talent which falls short of the 'super-being' which her fans would have us believe she is.

The clever way she has positioned herself in the business means that she could remain one of the top international celebrities for many years to come. Her talent is not transient. She has every reason to feel fulfilled, but the comparatively moderate impact she has had on the big screen, despite *Cabaret*, must be a source of disappointment and regret. Yet is it not to be expected with the kind of films now being made and the inevitable passing of time, for in other circumstances Liza could so easily by now have been a grandmother! The cinema is virtually the only part of her career which she has found difficult to handle. To achieve more in Hollywood terms has always meant a lot to her because her achievements so far must have fallen well short of her ambitions. Much of this is certainly because she finds it hard to compromise on standards and she is single-minded in what she wants. She once told *Film Review*: 'After *Cabaret* I waited three years for a really good woman's role to come along. Sure, I'm lucky because I can afford to wait and pick and choose ... I have my singing which brings in an income, totally independent of my acting.' But there is no mistaking her disappointment and frustration because she probably genuinely believes she could do more than just sing and dance. Convincing movie-makers is another matter.

So will the 1990s bring the chance for Liza Minnelli to consolidate and advance her status as a movie actress? It will continue to depend on the material available to her and whether public taste once again realigns with the film musical. Liza is unlikely to move back to the big screen just for the sake of it. The role would have to provide the right challenge. Should anyone like Andrew Lloyd Webber or Tim Rice ever become seriously involved with film, then openings might occur: Tim Rice, in fact, recently mentioned that Liza was screen-tested to play Evita in the early 1980s. Lewis Gilbert is certainly a Minnelli fan, and could perhaps be tempted back by the opportunity to work with her again in the right type of film vehicle, even though approaching his mid-eighties.

The ultimate opportunity, of course, would arise should some courageous soul decide to make a film based on the life of Judy Garland, because who would be better to portray her mother than Liza? Liza, though, has always been adamant that she would never get involved in any such project. She becomes so hostile at the possibility that one is left to wonder if it is not something which hovers menacingly in her sub-conscious, clouding the outer fringes of her life. She resolutely shuns Liza Minnelli biographies, even those that are friendly. She makes the clear distinction between that and journalism.

In 1989 she told *Observer Magazine*: 'In Hollywood now when people die they don't say, "Did he leave a will?", but, "Did he leave a diary"?' She abhors the idea of anyone using someone else's life to make money. How much more intense and frustrated would she become should her mother's life story on film be contemplated.

But on the other hand, if such a film *were* to be made anyway, would it not be better for Liza to be involved, to have some say in what is produced; even to handle and control the entire project herself perhaps, as Streisand did with *Yentl*?

Her critics and supporters alike would perhaps agree on Liza Minnelli's professionalism. She once told *Hello* magazine that she had never done anything professionally that she was ashamed of. 'I'm pleased with myself,' she said. 'By treating myself with respect, kindness and discipline, I've become my own best friend.' And when once asked about her ambitions she replied, grinning: 'I wanna do it all again — only better.'

As Mama would say . . . a real trouper.

Chronology

1945 Father (Vincente Minnelli) and mother (Judy Garland) marry (15 June).

1946 Born Tuesday, 12 March at Cedars of Lebanon Hospital, Hollywood.

1949 Makes movie debut at $2\frac{1}{2}$ years old in *In the Good Old Summertime*.

1951 As a 5-year-old sees mother's debut at the London Palladium (April).

1951 Appears as the Virgin Mary in school play.

1952 Mother and father divorced (March).

1952 Mother marries Sidney Luft (11 June).

1952 Lorna Luft born (21 November).

1954 As 6-year-old makes brief unbilled appearance in father's movie *The Long, Long, Trailer*.

1955 Joseph Wiley Luft (Joey) born (29 March).

1955 First television appearance, being interviewed on the *Art Linkletter Show*.

1956 Makes stage debut joining mother on stage at the Palace in New York to dance 'Swanee'.

1956 Second television appearance with host Bert Lahr.

1959 Appears with Gene Kelly in a duet and dancing ('Me and My Girl') on his television special (April).

1960 Appears on Hedda Hopper's Hollywood TV show (10 January) and sings 'Over the Rainbow'.

1960 Spends summer in France with party learning French.

1960 Attends High School of the Performing Arts (highlighted in the TV series Fame) in New York.

1961 Attends Scarsdale High School in New York.

1961 First real dramatic opportunity in *The Diary of Anne Frank*.

1962 Studies at the Sorbonne in Paris.

1962 Decides she wants to go into show business professionally. Moves on her own to New York with Broadway ambitions.

1962 Studies acting and voice production in New York.

1963 Appears on television's *Jack Paar Show* with her foot in plaster.

1963 *You Are For Loving*, first solo record, recorded (26 February).

1963 Appears in *Best Foot Forward* (April – September) in off-Broadway show.

1963 Wins the Daniel Blum Award for the year's most promising actress.

1963 Appears on television's *The Judy Garland Show*.

1964 Provides the voice of Dorothy in an animated sequel to *The Wizard of Oz*. Not shown in US until 1974. Released UK (minor) early 1973.

1964 Appears as Lili in stock company production of the musical *Carnival*.

1964 Co-stars with Judy in two concerts at the London Palladium.

1964 First appearance on British television (18 June) in The Cliff Richard Show.

1964 First solo record *You Are For Loving* released.

1964 First album released *Liza! Liza!* (December).

1965 On tour with The Fantasticks with Elliott Gould.

1965 Opens (11 May) in *Flora, The Red Menace* at the Alvin Theatre, New York. Performance secures a Tony Award as Best Musical Actress of the Year; at nineteen the youngest recipient of the award.

1965 Unsuccessful in bid to play Sally Bowles in the Broadway production of *Cabaret*.

1965 Starts out with her own act in nightclubs in the USA, Canada, London and Paris.

1965 Mother divorces Sidney Luft and marries Mark Herron (November).

1966 Cabaret debut appearance (February) at New York's Plaza Hotel's Persian Room a sell-out success.

1966 Nightclub appearances include Talk of the Town in London and the Coconut Grove in Los Angeles.

1966 Capital album *There is a Time* selected Best Album of the Year by Hi-Fi Stereo Review Magazine.

1967 Marries Peter Allen in New York (3 March).

1968 Features in cameo role in first feature film, *Charlie Bubbles*, starring Albert Finney.

1968 Successful opening (January) at New York's Waldorf Astoria's Empire Rooms.

1968 Three-week engagement at the Chequer's Club in Sydney, Australia.

1969 Stars in *The Sterile Cuckoo* (*Pookie* in UK). Performance receives an Oscar nomination.

1969 Mother marries Mickey Deans (15 March).

1969 Mother dies in London (22 June) from accidental drug overdose. Funeral 27 June.

1969 Appears at the Olympia, Paris.

1970 Stars in her third feature film *Tell Me That You Love Me, Junie Moon*.

1972 Stars as Sally Bowles in the film version of *Cabaret*. Receives both an Oscar and a Golden Globe for her performance.

1972 *Liza With a Z*, a television special, is filmed (31 May) before a live audience at New York's Lyceum Theatre (aired 10 September). Receives an Emmy.

1972 Named as one of the Ten Best Dressed Women in the world.

1973 Gives three performances of her one-woman show *Liza With a Z* at the London Palladium, Festival Hall and the Rainbow Theatre.

1974 Three-week engagement at the Winter Garden Theatre, New York (January), breaks Broadway records and secures a special Tony Award.

1974 Guest star and narrator in *That's Entertainment*, a movie tribute to MGM musicals.

1974 Appears at the Riviera in Las Vegas in a two-week sell-out engagement.

1974 Divorces Peter Allen (July) and marries Jack Haley Jnr (15 September).

1975 Stars in the film *Lucky Lady* with Burt Reynolds and Gene Hackman.

1975 Appears as Roxi Hart in the Broadway show *Chicago* for five weeks (August), standing in for Gwen Verdon who was sick.

1976 Features in *That's Entertainment Part 2*.

1976 Stars in the films *A Matter of Time* (directed by father) — never released in UK — and *Silent Movie*.

1976 Voted top box office draw for 1975 by Box Office Magazine.

1977 Stars in the film *New York, New York* with Robert De Niro.

1977 Stars on Broadway (October – July 1978) as Michelle Craig in *The Act* at the Majestic Theatre. *The Act* takes Broadway by storm with New Year's Eve performance a 'one-night' record-breaker.

1978 Concluding a European tour appears at the London Palladium (4 – 9 December) and the Olympia Theatre, Paris (17 – 18 December).

1978 Divorce from Jack Haley Jnr (December).

1979 Receives Tony Award (June) for her performance in the Broadway show, *The Act*.

1979 Plays Lillian Hellman in *Are You Now Or Have You Ever Been?* in New York for three weeks (January).

1979 Narrates *The Owl and the Pussy Cat* (July) for the Martha Graham Dance Company at the Royal Opera House, Covent Garden in London.

1979 Engagement *Liza in Concert at Carnegie Hall*, New York (September) — her first appearance at the venue — breaks box office records.

1979 *Goldie and Liza Together* made (October) by CBS.

1979 Marries Mark Gero (4 December).

1980 *Goldie and Liza Together* aired (19 February) by CBS.

1980 Appears as guest in the outstandingly successful *Baryshnikov on Broadway* on television (24 April, USA).

1981 Features in the film *Arthur* with Dudley Moore and Sir John Gielgud.

1983 Appears as a cardboard image in the film *The King of Comedy*.

1984 Reunites with her *Chicago* co-star for Kander and Ebb Broadway musical *The Rink* (9 February). Receives Tony nomination.

1984 Appears in a cameo role in *The Muppets Take Manhattan*.

1984 Checks into The Betty Ford Clinic.

1985 Features as narrator in the film *That's Dancin'*.

1986 Receives Golden Globe Award for Best Actress for dramatic performance in television presentation of *A Time to Live* (aired 28 October 1985) based on the best-selling book by Mary Lou Weisman.

1986 Father Vincente Minnelli dies (25 July).

1987 *Minnelli on Minnelli*, televised tribute to her father, broadcast (18 March).

1987 Sets new record for Carnegie Hall with longest continuous engagement (28 May to 18 June) in the hall's 96-year history.

1987 Series of concerts at London's Royal Albert Hall (November).

1988 Stars in the film *Rent-A-Cop* with Burt Reynolds.

1988 Visits England for a concert at the London Palladium, also recorded for TV.

1988 Appears with Dudley Moore and Sir John Gielgud in film *Arthur 2: On the Rocks.*

1988 New series *Frank, Liza and Sammy, The Ultimate Event* on tour.

1988 Makes major debut in American television commercial.

1988 *Liza Minnelli: Triple Play* (May), her first TV drama for two years.

1989 New album *Results* with The Pet Shop Boys receives Gold Disc in the UK.

1989 Stars with Frank Sinatra and Sammy Davis Jnr in London with *The Ultimate Event.*

1989 Appears on American TV at the Songwriters' Hall of Fame 20th Anniversary Show.

1990 Long-time friend Halston dies of AIDS (26 March).

1990 Sammy Davis Jnr dies of cancer (16 May).

1991 Stars in the film *Stepping Out* with Julie Walters and Shelley Winters. Royal world premiere in London (September).

1991 Liza Minnelli star unveiled on the Hollywood Walk of Fame.

1992 Divorce from Mark Gero (January).

1992 Leads a *Tribute to Sammy Davis Jnr* charity concert at London's Royal Albert Hall. Some £600,000 was raised.

1992 Death of former husband Peter Allen (June).

1992 Release in UK on video and audio of *Liza 'Live' from Radio City Music Hall*, her 1991 concert which broke all previous box-office records at the famous venue.

1993 Extensive concert series with Charles Aznavour through June, August and October.

1993 Concert with Frank Sinatra in New Jersey (December).

1993 Recording of 'The Day after That' from *Kiss of the Spiderwoman* for release in US (December) with proceeds for AIDS research.

Filmography

In the Good Old Summertime (US) 1949 MGM
Directed by Robert Z Leonard. Appeared as a toddler with her real mother, Judy Garland, and Van Johnson. Spring Byington and Buster Keaton were also in the cast.
Colour. 102 minutes.

The Long, Long Trailer (US) 1954 MGM
Directed by Vincente Minnelli. As a 6-year-old made a brief, unbilled appearance in her father's movie. Cast included Lucille Ball, Desi Arnaz, Marjorie Man and Keenan Wynn.
Colour. 96 minutes.

Journey Back to Oz (US). Also *Return to the Land Of Oz*.
Filmed 1964 (released US 1974, minor release UK early 1973) Norm Prescott and Lou Scheimer/Filmation. Directed

by Hal Sutherland. Provided the voice of Dorothy in a return journey over the rainbow in a cartoon version of Frank Baunm themes from *The Wizard of Oz*. Voice cast included Milton Berle, Ethel Merman, Mickey Rooney, Danny Thomas and Mel Blanc.
Colour. 90 minutes.

Charlie Bubbles (GB) 1968
Universal/Memorial
Directed by Albert Finney. Appeared in a cameo role as Eliza in her first feature film. Cast included Albert Finney, Billie Whitelaw, Colin Blakely, Timothy Garland, Peter Sallis, Diana Coupland, Wendy Padbury, Joe Gladwin and Bryan Moseley.
Colour. 89 minutes.

The Sterile Cuckoo (US).
Pookie in the UK. 1969 Paramount
Directed by Alan J Pakula. Appeared with Tim McIntire, Wendell Burton, Austin Green and Sandra Faison.
Colour. 107 minutes.
Liza Minnelli received an Oscar nomination.

Tell Me That You Love Me, Junie Moon
(US) 1970 Paramount/Sigma.
Directed by Otto Preminger. Appeared
with Ken Howard, Kay Thompson,
Leonard Frey, James Coco and Fred
Williamson.
Colour. 113 minutes.

Cabaret (US) 1972
ABC Pictures/Allied Artists
Directed and choreographed by Bob
Fosse. Appeared with Michael York,
Helmut Griem, Joel Grey, Fritz Wepper,
Marisa Berenson, Elisabeth Neumann-
Viertel and Sigrid Von Richthofen. Songs:
'Willkommen', 'Mein Herr', 'Two Ladies',
'Maybe This Time', 'Money Money
Money', 'If You Could See Her Through
My Eyes', 'Tomorrow Belongs to Me',
'Cabaret'.
Colour. 123 minutes.
Liza Minnelli received an Oscar for
Best Actress. Other main Oscars were
awarded to Joel Grey (Best Actor), Bob
Fosse (Director), Geoffrey Unsworth
(Photography), Ralph Burns (Musical
Director) and Herbert Strabel (Art
Director).

That's Entertainment (US) 1974 MGM
Directed by Jack Haley Jnr.
Featured as one of a host of Hollywood stars who narrate extracts from the musical films made by the studio which specialized in them.
Colour. 137 minutes.

Lucky Lady (US) 1975
TCF/Gruskoff/Venture
Directed by Stanley Donen. Appeared with Burt Reynolds, Gene Hackman, Michael Hordern, Geoffrey Lewis and Robby Benson.
Colour. 118 minutes.

That's Entertainment Part 2 (US) 1976 MGM
Directed by Gene Kelly.
Featured once more with a host of Hollywood stars who narrate extracts from the musical films made by MGM.
Colour. 133 minutes.

A Matter of Time (US/Italy) 1976
AIP/Jack H Skirball, J Edmund Grainger.
(Never released in the UK).
Directed by Vincente Minnelli. Appeared

with Ingrid Bergman, Charles Boyer, Tina Aumont, Gabriele Ferzetti and Spiros Andros. Songs: 'A Matter of Time', 'Do it Again', 'The Me I Haven't Met Yet'.
Colour. 97 minutes (originally 165 minutes).

Silent Movie (US) 1976 TCF/Crossbow Directed by Mel Brooks. Appeared as a guest star only along with Anne Bancroft, Paul Newman, Burt Reynolds, James Caan and Marcel Marceau.
Colour. 87 minutes.

New York, New York (US) 1977 United Artists/Chartoff-Winkler.
Directed by Martin Scorsese. Appeared with Robert De Niro, Lionel Stander and Barry Primus.
Songs (all sung by Liza Minnelli): 'You Brought a New Kind Of Love To Me', 'Once in a While', 'You Are My Lucky Star', 'The Man I Love', 'Just You Just Me', 'There Goes the Ball Game', 'Happy Endings', 'But the World Goes Round', 'New York, New York'.
Colour. 153 minutes.

Arthur (US) 1981 Warner/Orion.
Directed by Steve Gordon. Appeared with Dudley Moore, John Gielgud, Geraldine Fitzgerald, Jill Eikenberry and Stephen Elliott.
Colour. 97 minutes.

The King of Comedy (US) 1982 TCF/Embassy International.
Directed by Martin Scorsese. Only a cardboard image of Liza Minnelli was seen in this movie.
Colour. 109 minutes.

The Muppets Take Manhattan (US) 1984 Tri-Star.
Directed by Frank Oz. Appeared in a cameo role and said only a few words.
Colour. 94 minutes.

That's Dancin' (US) 1985 MGM-UA/David Niven Jnr, Jack Haley Jnr.
Directed by David Niven Jnr and Jack Haley Jnr. Liza Minnelli joins Gene Kelly, Sammy Davis Jnr, Mikhail Baryshnikov and Ray Bolger as a narrator in selections from the world of the movie musical.
Colour. 105 minutes.

Rent-A-Cop (US) 1988
Kings Road Entertainment.
Directed by Jerry London. Appeared with Burt Reynolds, James Remar, Bernie Casey, Richard Masur, Dionne Warwick and Robby Benson.
Colour. 97 minutes.

Arthur 2: On the Rocks (US) 1988
Warner/Orion.
Directed by Bud Yorkin. Appeared with Dudley Moore, Geraldine Fitzgerald, Paul Benedict, John Gielgud, Kathy Bates, Cynthia Sikes and Stephen Elliott.
Colour. 108 minutes.

Stepping Out (US) 1991 UIP/Paramount
Directed by Lewis Gilbert. Appears with Shelley Winters, Julie Walters, Robyn Stevan, Jane Krakowski, Bill Irwin, Ellen Greene, Sheila McCarthy, Andrea Martin, Carol Woods and Luke Reilly. Songs sung by Liza Minnelli: 'Stepping Out' and 'Mean To Me'.
Colour. 110 minutes.

Albums

(except compilation albums)

Material currently available in UK

The Act original Broadway cast (LP, cassette and CD)

(*The Act* has been re-released on two budget label CDs, 'Success' and 'Tring', neither explaining what *The Act* was, and just titled *Liza Minnelli The Act*, but both are exactly like the original Broadway soundtrack).

New York, New York original film soundtrack (LPs, cassette and CD)

The Rink Broadway cast (LP, cassette and CD)

Liza Minnelli 'Live' at Carnegie Hall '87 (LPs and CD)

Results (LP, cassette and CD)

Stepping Out original film soundtrack (LP, cassette and CD)

Cabaret original film soundtrack (LP, cassette and CD)

The Singer (LP, cassette and CD)

Liza With a Z (LP, cassette and CD)
Flora, The Red Menace (LP and CD)

Material issued but not currently available in UK
Liza, Liza (LP)
Best Foot Forward (LP)
Judy Garland and Liza Minnelli 'Live' at the London Palladium (LPs)
It Amazes Me (LP)
The Dangerous Christmas of Red Riding Hood (LP) (TV cast album)
There is a Time (LP and cassette)
Liza Minnelli (LP and cassette)
Come Saturday Morning (LP and cassette)
New Feelin' (LP and cassette)
Liza Minnelli 'Live' at the Winter Garden (LP and cassette)
Liza Minnelli Foursider (LPs, cassette and CD)
Portrait of Liza Minnelli (LPs) (British four-sider release with additional tracks)
Liza Minnelli 'Live' at the Olympia in Paris (LP, cassette and CD)
Lucky Lady original film soundtrack (LP)
Nina original film soundtrack (*A Matter of Time*) (LP)

Tropical Nights (LP, cassette and CD)
Liza Minnelli 'Live' at Carnegie Hall '79
   (LPs) (Australian release through RCA
   cassette and LP)

Notes

There were singles released from the
Results album, but all have now been
deleted, though on occasion they can
still be found in record shops.

CDs are always being released of old
albums so these are sometimes available
in certain shops, especially on American
import and Japanese import.

Albums re-released, but with one or two
tracks missing from the original (though
these are not currently available in the
UK) are: *There is a Time* ('One of
These Songs' track missing); *Maybe This
Time* (re-release of *Liza, Liza* with 'Blue
Moon' and 'I'm All I've Got' tracks
missing).

Compilation albums made up of other pre-release albums

Currently available
Judy and Liza at the Palladium (LP and CD)
I Believe in Music (cassette)
Lovely Liza Minnelli (cassette)

Currently not available
Some of Those Songs (CD) (Australian release of 1960s albums)
Encore (LP)
American Superstars (LP)
The Liza Minnelli Collection (LP) (Australian '81 tour release)
Portrait of Liza (LP) (Reader's Digest release)

Videos

A Time to Live Castle Vision video

An Evening With Liza Minnelli (live in New Orleans 1979) EMI video

Arthur Warner Bros video

Arthur 2: On the Rocks Warner Bros video

Cabaret Rank video (now available on Spotlight video)

Frank, Sammy and Liza The video collection Kodak video programs

Journey Back to Oz Castle Vision video

Liza Minnelli 'Live' from Radio City Music Hall SMV video

New York, New York United Artists video

Princess and the Pea MGM/UA video

Rent-A-Cop Vestro Video International

Stepping Out CIC video

Visible Results CMV video

No other pre-recorded films of Liza Minnelli are currently available in the UK.

Other titles in the
Ulverscroft Large Print Series:

TO FIGHT THE WILD
Rod Ansell and Rachel Percy

Lost in uncharted Australian bush, Rod Ansell survived by hunting and trapping wild animals, improvising shelter and using all the bushman's skills he knew.

COROMANDEL
Pat Barr

India in the 1830s is a hot, uncomfortable place, where the East India Company still rules. Amelia and her new husband find themselves caught up in the animosities which seethe between the old order and the new.

THE SMALL PARTY
Lillian Beckwith

A frightening journey to safety begins for Ruth and her small party as their island is caught up in the dangers of armed insurrection.

THE WILDERNESS WALK
Sheila Bishop

Stifling unpleasant memories of a misbegotten romance in Cleave with Lord Francis Aubrey, Lavinia goes on holiday there with her sister. The two women are thrust into a romantic intrigue involving none other than Lord Francis.

THE RELUCTANT GUEST
Rosalind Brett

Ann Calvert went to spend a month on a South African farm with Theo Borland and his sister. They both proved to be different from her first idea of them, and there was Storr Peterson — the most disturbing man she had ever met.

ONE ENCHANTED SUMMER
Anne Tedlock Brooks

A tale of mystery and romance and a girl who found both during one enchanted summer.

CLOUD OVER MALVERTON
Nancy Buckingham

Dulcie soon realises that something is seriously wrong at Malverton, and when violence strikes she is horrified to find herself under suspicion of murder.

AFTER THOUGHTS
Max Bygraves

The Cockney entertainer tells stories of his East End childhood, of his RAF days, and his post-war showbusiness successes and friendships with fellow comedians.

MOONLIGHT
AND MARCH ROSES
D. Y. Cameron

Lynn's search to trace a missing girl takes her to Spain, where she meets Clive Hendon. While untangling the situation, she untangles her emotions and decides on her own future.

NURSE ALICE IN LOVE
Theresa Charles

Accepting the post of nurse to little Fernie Sherrod, Alice Everton could not guess at the romance, suspense and danger which lay ahead at the Sherrod's isolated estate.

POIROT INVESTIGATES
Agatha Christie

Two things bind these eleven stories together — the brilliance and uncanny skill of the diminutive Belgian detective, and the stupidity of his Watson-like partner, Captain Hastings.

LET LOOSE THE TIGERS
Josephine Cox

Queenie promised to find the long-lost son of the frail, elderly murderess, Hannah Jason. But her enquiries threatened to unlock the cage where crucial secrets had long been held captive.

THE TWILIGHT MAN
Frank Gruber

Jim Rand lives alone in the California desert awaiting death. Into his hermit existence comes a teenage girl who blows both his past and his brief future wide open.

DOG IN THE DARK
Gerald Hammond

Jim Cunningham breeds and trains gun dogs, and his antagonism towards the devotees of show spaniels earns him many enemies. So when one of them is found murdered, the police are on his doorstep within hours.

THE RED KNIGHT
Geoffrey Moxon

When he finds himself a pawn on the chessboard of international espionage with his family in constant danger, Guy Trent becomes embroiled in moves and countermoves which may mean life or death for Western scientists.

TIGER TIGER
Frank Ryan

A young man involved in drugs is found murdered. This is the first event which will draw Detective Inspector Sandy Woodings into a whirlpool of murder and deceit.

CAROLINE MINUSCULE
Andrew Taylor

Caroline Minuscule, a medieval script, is the first clue to the whereabouts of a cache of diamonds. The search becomes a deadly kind of fairy story in which several murders have an other-worldly quality.

LONG CHAIN OF DEATH
Sarah Wolf

During the Second World War four American teenagers from the same town join the Army together. Forty-two years later, the son of one of the soldiers realises that someone is systematically wiping out the families of the four men.

THE LISTERDALE MYSTERY
Agatha Christie

Twelve short stories ranging from the light-hearted to the macabre, diverse mysteries ingeniously and plausibly contrived and convincingly unravelled.

TO BE LOVED
Lynne Collins

Andrew married the woman he had always loved despite the knowledge that Sarah married him for reasons of her own. So much heartache could have been avoided if only he had known how vital it was to be loved.

ACCUSED NURSE
Jane Converse

Paula found herself accused of a crime which could cost her her job, her nurse's reputation, and even the man she loved, unless the truth came to light.

A GREAT DELIVERANCE
Elizabeth George

Into the web of old houses and secrets of Keldale Valley comes Scotland Yard Inspector Thomas Lynley and his assistant to solve a particularly savage murder.

'E' IS FOR EVIDENCE
Sue Grafton

Kinsey Millhone was bogged down on a warehouse fire claim. It came as something of a shock when she was accused of being on the take. She'd been set up. Now she had a new client — herself.

A FAMILY OUTING IN AFRICA
Charles Hampton and Janie Hampton

A tale of a young family's journey through Central Africa by bus, train, river boat, lorry, wooden bicycle and foot.

THE PLEASURES OF AGE
Robert Morley

The author, British stage and screen star, now eighty, is enjoying the pleasures of age. He has drawn on his experiences to write this witty, entertaining and informative book.

THE VINEGAR SEED
Maureen Peters

The first book in a trilogy which follows the exploits of two sisters who leave Ireland in 1861 to seek their fortune in England.

A VERY PAROCHIAL MURDER
John Wainwright

A mugging in the genteel seaside town turned to murder when the victim died. Then the body of a young tearaway is washed ashore and Detective Inspector Lyle is determined that a second killing will not go unpunished.

DEATH ON A HOT SUMMER NIGHT
Anne Infante

Micky Douglas is either accident-prone or someone is trying to kill him. He finds himself caught in a desperate race to save his ex-wife and others from a ruthless gang.

HOLD DOWN A SHADOW
Geoffrey Jenkins

Maluti Rider, with the help of four of the world's most wanted men, is determined to destroy the Katse Dam and release a killer flood.

THAT NICE MISS SMITH
Nigel Morland

A reconstruction and reassessment of the trial in 1857 of Madeleine Smith, who was acquitted by a verdict of Not Proven of poisoning her lover, Emile L'Angelier.

SEASONS OF MY LIFE
Hannah Hauxwell
and Barry Cockcroft

The story of Hannah Hauxwell's struggle to survive on a desolate farm in the Yorkshire Dales with little money, no electricity and no running water.

TAKING OVER
Shirley Lowe and Angela Ince

A witty insight into what happens when women take over in the boardroom and their husbands take over chores, children and chickenpox.

AFTER MIDNIGHT STORIES,
The Fourth Book Of

A collection of sixteen of the best of today's ghost stories, all different in style and approach but all combining to give the reader that special midnight shiver.

DEATH TRAIN
Robert Byrne

The tale of a freight train out of control and leaking a paralytic nerve gas that turns America's West into a scene of chemical catastrophe in which whole towns are rendered helpless.

THE ADVENTURE OF THE CHRISTMAS PUDDING
Agatha Christie

In the introduction to this short story collection the author wrote "This book of Christmas fare may be described as 'The Chef's Selection'. I am the Chef!"

RETURN TO BALANDRA
Grace Driver

Returning to her Caribbean island home, Suzanne looks forward to being with her parents again, but most of all she longs to see Wim van Branden, a coffee planter she has known all her life.

SKINWALKERS
Tony Hillerman

The peace of the land between the sacred mountains is shattered by three murders. Is a 'skinwalker', one who has rejected the harmony of the Navajo way, the murderer?

A PARTICULAR PLACE
Mary Hocking

How is Michael Hoath, newly arrived vicar of St. Hilary's, to meet the demands of his flock and his strained marriage? Further complications follow when he falls hopelessly in love with a married parishioner.

A MATTER OF MISCHIEF
Evelyn Hood

A saga of the weaving folk in 18th century Scotland. Physician Gavin Knox was desperately seeking a cure for the pox that ravaged the slums of Glasgow and Paisley, but his adored wife, Margaret, stood in the way.